In Search of Worship

John Clements

O&U
Onwards & Upwards

Onwards and Upwards Publishers

4 The Old Smithy, London Road, Rockbeare,
EX5 2EA, United Kingdom.
www.onwardsandupwards.org

Copyright © John Clements 2022

The moral right of John Clements to be identified as the author of this work has been asserted by the author in accordance with the Copyright, Designs and Patents Act 1988.

All rights reserved.

No part of this publication may be reproduced or transmitted in any form or by any means, electronic or mechanical, including photocopy, recording or any information storage and retrieval system, without permission in writing from the author or publisher.

First edition, published in the United Kingdom by Onwards and Upwards Publishers (2022).

ISBN: 978-1-78815-900-5
Typeface: Sabon LT

Unless otherwise stated, Scripture quotations are taken from the Amplified® Bible, Copyright © 1954, 1958, 1962, 1964, 1965, 1987 by The Lockman Foundation. Used by permission. www.Lockman.org

Scripture quotations marked (KJV) are from The Authorized (King James) Version. Rights in the Authorized Version in the United Kingdom are vested in the Crown. Reproduced by permission of the Crown's patentee, Cambridge University Press.

Scripture quotations marked (NCV) are taken from the New Century Version®. Copyright © 2005 by Thomas Nelson. Used by permission. All rights reserved.

Scripture quotations marked (NKJV) are taken from the New King James Version®. Copyright © 1982 by Thomas Nelson. Used by permission. All rights reserved.

In this book, John Clements highlights energetic seeds which, if received into fertile soil rather than places trodden down by convention, have the power to transform and revive both individual and corporate expressions of love for God.

Its pages will encourage apostles to re-examine founding principles, prophets to gain a wider context for what they see, evangelists to be motivated by the worship-potential in every human being, pastors to reconnect with the biblical direction of travel and teachers to search beneath the commonplace.

All individuals that comprise the biblical priesthood can find clarity here regarding the overarching purpose of their lives, whilst discovering that the keys to physical, mental and spiritual health, set out long ago in the scriptures, can hold true for them personally today.

For those who seek more than the acquisition or affirmation of knowledge, this book will enlighten an exciting journey of discovery towards "God with us".

The Worship Alliance

Acknowledgements

As in the natural, the body of Christ has many parts, each contributing to the smooth functioning of the whole, and the production of this book is no exception.

The seeds were planted over a period of years when the author was privileged to spend time worshipping with others whose hearts burned to bring offerings of praise and worship to their Lord, often at considerable personal cost. Their names, like many of those whom King David appointed to oversee worship, are recorded in heaven, and their worship has inspired some of the insights in this book.

Credit is also due to my publishers, Onwards and Upwards, and in particular to Luke Jeffery, who has tirelessly encouraged and guided me through the process of publication. His godly advice, insights, corrections, suggestions and patience have been invaluable. No-one could have wished for more supportive publishers.

Special thanks also to my wife and the few close friends who have often encouraged me when I needed it, and made helpful suggestions.

Credit, ultimately and obviously, must go to the Lord, for allowing (and encouraging) us to experience special times in His presence, when the Holy Spirit has inspired and instructed us as we have sought to bring our offerings of worship.

Contents

1. Introduction 1
2. Why Should We Worship God? 7
3. Worship in the Old Testament 15
4. Worship Under the Law 19
5. David's Tabernacle 26
6. David – The Shepherd Who Became King 30
7. The Key of David 35
8. The Psalms 38
9. Other Old Testament Examples 42
10. Worship in the New Testament 44
11. The Songs We Sing 54
12. What Happens When We Worship? 62
13. What Motivates Our Worship? 68
14. Hindrances and Opposition 72
15. Unity is Important 78
16. Worship Can Be Expensive! 81
17. Worship and Tithing 84
18. For His Glory Alone 89
19. "Me a Priest? Surely Not!" 92
20. What is the Purpose of Church? 96
21. Which Jesus Will You Worship? 104
22. Progression in Worship 108
23. The Use and Misuse of Music 112
24. Cultural Contexts 122
25. Evangelism or Worship? 125
26. Summary and Conclusion 130

1

Introduction

This book is about worship.

You may want to ask yourself why you have chosen to read it.

Are you looking for fresh inspiration?

Perhaps you are just curious, wondering why a whole book focusses on worship.

There are other books about worship – and there are also endless books of Christian hymns and songs which are loosely referred to as 'songs of worship'.

But what do we mean by worship?

More importantly, what does God expect when He invites His children to worship Him?

†

Our understanding of worship will inevitably be incomplete until we bow before the throne of our awesome God – "lost in wonder, love, and praise", to quote an old hymn[1].

Until then we can have only a partial understanding, and limited experience, of worship, but there are heights and depths to be touched which relatively few believers seem to experience.

So, the purpose of this book is to encourage us all to explore the eternal dimensions of spiritual worship – for one reason only, which is that *our Lord is worth it!*

Here are some questions:

- Are our church structures conducive to worship?

---

[1] 'Love divine, all loves excelling'

Introduction

- Do the times in which we live make worship particularly difficult?
- Should churches focus more on evangelism than worship?
- Is worship being actively discouraged by our enemy because it offends him?

This book will explore these and other issues.

The Words We Use

We often need to define what we mean by the words we use. As the English language develops over time, some words fall out of use and others attract entirely different meanings. At the present time it is unusual to hear a sentence without the words 'like' and 'so'! In this age of electronic gadgets, many words take on new meanings – for example, 'ram', 'driver', 'cloud', 'visit', 'boot', and many more. For those of a certain generation, this can sometimes be confusing!

This can be equally true for those of us who use a Christian vocabulary. Words like 'church', 'fellowship', and 'believe' can mean different things to different people, even if we know roughly what they describe. And perhaps one of the least understood Christian words is 'worship'.

Many churches display an invitation to join their "Morning Worship" – traditionally at 11am! – but the content of those services can vary enormously, and may include any of the following:

hymn-singing	recitations
preaching	personal testimonies
taking communion	talent spots
teaching	liturgical sequences
prayer	international news updates
discussion	drama
singing by a choir collecting money	children's activities

The list could go on…

All legitimate aspects of corporate worship, you may think.

Some people would also class social action as a part of their worship – caring for the sick and homeless, welcoming refugees, contributing to the relief of international poverty, addressing injustice and funding Christian charities. All part of serving a God Who hates suffering, loves everyone and expects us to work on His behalf in this dark world. These, surely, constitute valid aspects of our worship.

Others consider their worship to be their Christian lifestyle, i.e. living in a God-honouring way constitutes worship; worship is about who we are and not what we do; worship is defined by the lives we live.

Yet others consider regular church attendance to be their worship.

The Questions Keep Coming

- Are there constant factors in the worship of believers through the ages?
- Is it valid to express worship differently in different cultures?
- Why do people worship anyway?
- Should everyone be a worshipper?
- Did worship mean the same to St Paul as it did to Abraham?
- Was worship primarily an old covenant requirement?
- If people choose not to worship God, is that acceptable to Him?
- Will our status in heaven be affected by our worship choices while on earth?

In many cultures, men worship to win the favour of their deity. But if our salvation depends on Christ's finished work at the cross and not on what we do, maybe all we have to do is relax and wait for heaven? (Lest you cry "Heresy!" at this point, be assured that this is not the conclusion of this book!)

Worship is Not Exclusively a Christian Activity

This hardly needs to be said.

As hinted above, most primitive religions involve the worship of spirits or deities – usually out of fear. To win the favour of their gods, devotees may engage in all manner of ceremonies, often involving trances, self-mutilation, sacrifices and elaborate rituals.

Introduction

Throughout history, dictators have often demanded adulation and worship – sometimes with severe penalties for those who refused to acquiesce. A clear example would be the Babylonian king Nebuchadnezzar, who demanded unconditional worship from all his subjects and whose reign came to an abrupt end because of that idolatry [Dan.3:5-7; 4:25.33]. More recently, mass adulation was demanded by Nazi leaders at public gatherings – perhaps most notably at Nuremburg.

In modern times, many top footballers and pop stars enjoy the exuberant public worship of their fans, demonstrated by singing, chanting and hand-waving.

It seems that our Creator has built into mankind the capacity and desire to worship, and that this gets expressed in many ways and focusses on many things.

Worship is Not Limited to Time and Space

The first dispute in eternity, long before God created man, concerned the issue of worship. Satan, who many believe was the archangel responsible for worship in heaven, chose to divert that worship away from God to himself. For that reason, and for that reason alone, he was ejected from heaven and God's presence [Ezek.28:13-17; Is.14:12-15].

His mission ever since has been to prevent man from worshipping God, and to establish an alternative kingdom in which only he, Satan, would be worshipped. The end time revelations in the last book of the Bible confirm that this is his ultimate goal.

His ultimate coup, had he succeeded, would have been to persuade Jesus to worship him during the gruelling temptation in the wilderness [Lk.4]. If successful, he would have had legitimate control of world events from that point on, with unthinkable consequences. Thankfully, Jesus resisted the temptation to trade worshipping Satan for the satisfaction of His personal needs.

More on that later, but it lays the foundation for much of what follows and underlines the cosmic significance of worship. It shows that in the context of eternity, worship must focus on God, and on Him alone.

Worship vs. Idolatry

The history of Israel is recorded in great detail in much of the Old Testament, and the nation's fortunes seem to rise and fall in direct proportion to whether their 'affiliation' is to God or to other deities and idols.

When they worshipped God they were blessed and successful. When they worshipped idols they suffered military defeats, poverty and came under God's judgement. The worship of idols also had negative consequences for individuals as well as nations, and we can presume that nothing has changed!

Throughout history, idolatry has taken many forms. Some have been blatant and very public. Some have been subtle and insidious. The study of idolatry is beyond the scope of this book, but the discovery of artifacts from past civilisations shows that man has always engaged in various ceremonies to win the approval of spirits or deities.

What constitutes idolatry in our contemporary culture may become clearer as we explore its converse – true worship.

What does it Mean – To Worship?

To attempt a definition, worship is an expression of devotion and respect to a deity.

The word comes from the Old English words 'worth' and 'ship', where 'worth' denotes the acknowledged merit of the person or deity being worshipped, and 'ship' denotes rank or status; hence, our English use of the word in a legal context: "Your Worship".

So, to worship God is to acknowledge Who He is, and describes our response to that knowledge with expressions of our devotion.

To *believe* in God is not the same as *worshipping* Him. Worshipping Him is essentially something we *do* and is not just about believing.

In other words, it is our volitional response, expressed to God, in recognition of Who He is and what He means to us.

Throughout the centuries, those who have had an encounter with Almighty God instinctively worship Him. It is not a legal requirement, but it is an almost inevitable human response to God's presence and glory.

2

Why Should We Worship God?

It is a valid question.

Does He not have enough worship from the heavenly beings? Clearly they do it a lot.

Surely their worship is far superior to anything we can produce on earth? What difference could it make to an Almighty God to have the worship of imperfect human beings?

The angelic beings probably have far superior talents and vocal skills! Surely God is worshipped enough already. What difference could we make?

†

In fact, the question "Why should we worship God?" is misplaced and unhelpful. In a loving human relationship we do not ask the question, "Why should I love you?" If you find yourself in love with someone – regardless of whether that person is already loved by others – that question would be irrelevant and probably met with the answer, "Because I do!"

And so it is in relation to God.

We can also say that the word 'should' itself is unhelpful. It has overtones of duty, of obedience, even of reluctant compliance, and has no place in the language of worship.

Some would argue that there is a 'should' in the first commandment. We can easily interpret this to mean that worshipping God is a legal requirement. The first commandment does indeed say, "You must..." but it is a "must *not*" and refers to idolatry. God does not command His people to love or worship Him. He prohibits them from worshipping idols but He knows that true worship can never be legally demanded; it is only meaningful when given voluntarily and out of love.

You cannot produce love by legislation!

†

So, returning to the question "Why should we worship God?", we can say that if there is a need to ask the 'should' question, there is probably a flaw in our understanding of God and our relationship with Him. There may even be a hint of escapism: "Maybe I won't have to deal with this if I can find reasons for *not* worshipping God…"

There are better questions to ask!

God has never demanded man's worship. However, He clearly desires it, loves it, encourages it – and actually rewards it, as we shall see. For reasons best known to Himself, He receives the praise and worship of human beings – perhaps because our worship springs from love and not duty.

The worship given by angelic beings is constant and not optional, and they have no experience of an environment where God is not worshipped. Whether they have a love for God, in the sense that we understand love, is unclear from scripture, but there is something special to God about the worship of those who have become His children by redemption and who express their love for Him in praise and worship.

But If You do Need Reasons…

Actually, we can answer the question "Why should we worship God?" in a more positive way. There are many *reasons* for worshipping God.

In short, they concern Who He is and what He has done.

Here are a few:

- He is entitled to be honoured above all things because He is above all things;
- He is worthy of the highest praise because He is perfect, majestic, merciful, loving and faithful;
- He is always good;

In Search of Worship

- He takes pleasure in those who revere Him [Ps.147:11];
- He created all things for His *"pleasure"* [Rev.4:11, see KJV], and, amazingly, we can contribute to His pleasure;
- He inhabits the praises of His people [Ps.22:3, see KJV].

†

So, you may agree that the question "Why should we?" slips away into irrelevance.

A better question would be, "When *can* we?"

Misconceptions

Perhaps one of the primary reasons for an unwillingness to engage in worship is an erroneous perception of the character of God.

If we have a distorted understanding of the nature of God, or if we doubt our own identity as His children, we will find worship difficult.

Here are a few common ones:

- God is usually disappointed with us because we do not live up to His standards or achieve what He expects of us, so we are reluctant to appear before Him because He must have 'issues' with us.
- God is super-holy and we are not, so He will surely not want us to get too close.
- Our function in His kingdom is primarily one of service for an absent master, and we're doing our best to keep busy until (or in case!) He comes back. That takes up most of our time, and of course He values our faithful service more than our worship (which is mostly about singing songs and not about getting things done).
- God will not value our miniscule offerings of worship because others do it better than we do, and also because He has the real stuff in heaven.
- God's priority is surely to get people 'saved' and into His kingdom. That must be more important to Him than singing songs.
- God is to be feared.

This last one is a big one.

Why Should We Worship God?

There are certainly many Bible verses telling us to fear God – and if we don't, there will be trouble! People also talk about 'putting the fear of God' into someone. We may even describe people as God-fearing – reinforcing the perception that some people are upright citizens because they are afraid of God.

There are verses like "The fear of the Lord is the beginning of wisdom" [Prov.1:7] and "Fear the Lord and turn away from evil" [Prov.3:7]. We may read such verses (and there are many), and be thinking, "Better be careful – He's obviously up there watching me, and there will be consequences if I mess up." In other words, God is someone to be afraid of and not someone you want to get too close to.

It is hard to worship what you fear!

But the problem is in our English language. There are different words for 'fear' in the original text – some implying 'terror', and others 'reverence and respect' – but many of our bibles use the word 'fear' without further clarification.

So verses like *"The fear of the Lord is the beginning of wisdom"* [Prov.1:7] can easily be misunderstood to mean 'be afraid of', rather than to 'revere' and 'honour'. The Amplified Version has a better translation: *"...the reverent and worshipful fear of the Lord is the beginning ... of knowledge..."*

This is about respecting Him, honouring Him and living with an awareness that He is worthy of our worship. If we understand that 'fearing the Lord' means we are to be afraid of Him, and therefore dread being in His presence, we shall be reluctant to draw near and worship Him.

If our image of God is that He is distant, unloving, demanding, critical, sin-hating and law-enforcing, we will not be keen to love or worship Him. After all, you don't love policemen or traffic wardens!

†

A distorted understanding of the nature of God can hinder our desire to offer Him worship.

In Search of Worship

It is hardly surprising, therefore, that Satan's mission from the beginning has been to discredit God's loving character and prevent us from approaching Him in worship.

This strategy was successful right from the beginning, when he persuaded Eve that God did not have her best interests at heart – saying, in effect, "If you ignore His instructions and make your own decisions, this will be to your advantage. Obviously, God is withholding the best from you."

He continues to paint distorted images of God to prevent us from having a loving relationship with Him, and to create barriers between us. He knows that Jesus' death and resurrection dealt with the issue of sin, and that we have been reconciled to God – but he still tries to convince us that God hates us (or at least disapproves of us) because we are sinful. Having this mindset will effectively kill any desire to worship God.

But we need to understand that, first and foremost, God is *for* us and not *against* us if we have trusted in His Son and His righteousness for our justification.

†

Of course, it was not always so.

You may remember that the Israelites were barred, on pain of death, from approaching Mount Sinai when God gave the Law to Moses. The message was clear: "If you cross the line to get close to God you will die." Even during the era of tabernacle worship, the people were strictly excluded from God's presence in the holy of holies.

God wanted to be in the midst of His people, but their sin prevented them from having close access to His presence. The same barrier to intimacy was enforced when Solomon built his magnificent temple. The people only had access to God through the priests, and were barred from the holy of holies.

Now, however, because of Jesus' perfect sacrifice for sin, there is no barrier to God's presence. In fact, quite the opposite is true: He *invites* us to approach Him. *"Let us then fearlessly and confidently … draw near"* [Heb.4:16].

The thick curtain in the temple, which protected God's holiness and kept sinful men away, was supernaturally ripped down when Jesus died. It was torn from the top – a clear indication that God accepted Jesus' sacrifice on our behalf and no longer needed to keep us out.

The way into His presence was opened, and has remained open, for us. We are now acceptable to God and may "draw near".

Of course, if we depend on our own righteousness to approach Him, we will inevitably feel unworthy because our best is never good enough!

The Scriptures tell us the good news that there is *"no condemnation ... for those who are in Christ Jesus"* [Rom.8.1], for we are no longer striving to be worthy by our own works (which will always fall short of God's standards). The righteousness that makes us acceptable to God is Christ's, not our own – and His righteousness ensures our welcome into God's presence at any time! This is pure grace, and is foundational to an understanding of our identity as we approach God in worship.

As we approach, we stand on holy ground – but not on ground we have created by our own merit!

So, contrary to Satan's lies, we are God's children and He loves us!

Is that hard to believe?

Look again at the story of Abraham and Isaac. Abraham (the father) has a son, a son he loves very much, and he is prepared to kill him in obedience to God's instructions. How much did Abraham love God? Enough to sacrifice the dearest possession he had – his son. How much does God love us? Enough to sacrifice His only Son, a Son He dearly loves, in order to buy us and include us in His family! Never believe the devil's lie that we are unloved by a God Who paid such a high price for a relationship with us!

†

We also need to understand the magnitude of God's long-term plan – which is not just about rescuing mankind from hell and getting more people into His kingdom. If you imagine lines of ragged saints waiting at heaven's gates with their 'saved by the blood of Jesus' passes in their hands, having just made it, and God looking on wondering if it was all worth it – you couldn't be more wrong!

His eternal purpose has been to unite a vast gathering of sparkling worshippers from every corner of the earth, from every tribe, every nationality and every language – and no doubt He is looking forward to the richness of our combined worship offerings, the like of which heaven has yet to see or hear [Rev.7:9-11]! Maybe you will be part of that throng? There is a hint of this momentous event in Malachi 3:16-17, where God says a day will come when He will publicly declare His *"jewels"* – His special treasures. And, according to this scripture, who will they be? They will be those who *"reverenced and worshipfully feared the Lord"*.

There will be a reversal of the chaos of Babel where proud men were trying to reach heaven by building a high tower, and where God frustrated their goal by multiplying their languages and causing their dispersion. In contrast, in heaven every tribe, nation and language will unite in praise.

This is way beyond the limited understanding of salvation which many have, and which sees redemption as focussing on its benefits to mankind. Salvation can easily be seen as 'man-centred' – an amazing rescue plan carried out at an unbelievable cost, but solely for the good of damaged mankind. But our salvation is not an entity in itself. God's purposes for us do not end once we are 'born again'. He weaves us into the vast tapestry of His eternal master plan, takes pleasure in us, and loves us beyond anything we can imagine.

Paul tries to explain the vastness of God's eternal plan and prays that the Ephesians will have insight into the mysteries of God – including *"how rich is His ... inheritance in the saints"* [Eph.1:18]!

Meditating on these marvels will help us to worship a God Who has amazing plans for us and takes great pleasure in us, His saints. This is the God we worship.

These are the facts that should help us to overcome any reluctance to worship, knowing that we are unconditionally loved and part of His amazing plans for eternity.

†

It is hardly surprising that because God inhabits the praise of His people, the enemy will do all he can to prevent the intrusion of his archenemy into what he sees as his territory.

Why Should We Worship God?

A brief look at some of his other tactics will be the subject of a later chapter[2].

---

[2] 'Hindrances and Opposition'; p.93.

3

Worship in the Old Testament

As always, the Scriptures are our guide when it comes to understanding spiritual things. A brief look at some of the instances of worship in Old Testament times is helpful.

The Bible also records many examples of idolatrous worship, into which even God's special people get drawn, and the results are usually disastrous – for both the nation and individuals.[3]

†

No instructions were given to Adam and Eve about worship.

Before the Fall [Gen.3], they enjoyed daily communion with God and presumably needed no instructions as to how to relate to Him. We do not read of any set procedures, special activities, or set times which characterised their relationship with God – although Genesis does record regular meetings *"in the cool of the day"* [Gen.3:8, NKJV]. Maybe in the context of that perfect relationship there would have been no concept of what we now call worship.

Early Examples of Worship

After the Fall, people began to approach God with gifts or offerings, although there is no record of God having demanded them.

"In the course of time, Cain brought the Lord an offering of the fruit of the ground. And Abel brought of the first-born of his flock" [Gen.4:3-4]. One offering was acceptable; the other was not. It seems that Abel brought the first and the best, while Cain just brought some of his vegetables! Even if there were no pre-existing instructions about

---

[3] For example, Ex.32:4,35, where Israel worshipped a golden calf; or 2Chr.25:14,27, where King Amaziah adopted the gods of the Edomites and incurred God's wrath.

acceptable offerings, God was obviously aware of the men's motives and could see into their hearts. Also, we now understand the significance of a 'blood offering' compared to one of fruit and veg!

It is interesting to note that after the birth of Adam's third child *"men began to call on the name of the Lord"* [Gen.4:26]. Sadly, no more details are given.

†

For several hundred years, little more is said about men making offerings to the Lord, although the practice may have continued.

Enoch and Noah are mentioned as God-fearing men, but neither is recorded as making sacrifices or offerings to God until after the Flood, when Noah built an altar and offered burnt offerings to the Lord – offerings which God accepted with pleasure.

†

Abraham also built altars and worshipped God:

- he built an altar in honour of the Lord [Gen.12:7];
- he built an altar in response to God's promises [Gen.13:18];
- he fell on his face before the Lord in response to God's promises [Gen.17:3].

Jacob also worshipped God:

- he set up a commemorative pillar to honour God's presence [Gen.28:18];
- he offered sacrifices to God [Gen.46:1].

Before Moses was instructed to set up the tabernacle, there were no detailed instructions about how the people were to worship – except that in Ex.20 we find God telling Moses to remind the people that whilst they were not to make or worship gods of silver or gold, they could make altars of earth or unhewn stone on which to offer their burnt and peace offerings. God also promised to bless the people in response to their sacrifices, wherever and whenever they were made [Ex.20:24].

Abraham

Abraham was well over a hundred years old when God set him a test – a test about his willingness to obey God at a very high personal cost. The test involved sacrificing his son to God as a burnt offering. Incredibly, Abraham was willing to comply, but God stepped in to prevent Isaac's death, and provided a substitute which Abraham then offered to God on the altar he had made. This seems to be an early example of acceptable worship, involving the offering to God of something precious – in Abraham's case, his much-loved son.

†

One of the fundamental principles of biblical exegesis concerns the significance of 'first mention'. This means it is worth noting the context of the first time a name, concept or phrase occurs.

The first mention of *"worship"* in Scripture is in Genesis 22, and concerns Abraham. He tells his two servants, *"Stay here with the donkey and I and the young man will go yonder and worship"* [Gen.22:5]. This is in response to God's instructions that he should take his son *"whom you love ... and offer him ... as a burnt offering on one of the mountains which I shall tell you"* [Gen.22.2, NKJV].

He takes a knife and some fire, and in a prophetic act, lays the wood on his son Isaac (surely foreshadowing the journey Jesus made to Golgotha); they then travel on to the appointed mountain. Isaac is clearly not surprised by his father's plans for a sacrificial offering, indicating that such offerings may have been made previously – his only surprise being the lack of a suitable animal for the burnt offering.

When questioned by Isaac, Abraham assures him, perhaps prophetically, that *"God Himself will provide a lamb"* [Gen.22:8], and as we now know, Isaac was spared and Abraham offered a ram on the altar he had made. We can only imagine the excruciating pain of a father contemplating the murder of his son, and perhaps also get a glimpse of God the Father's pain as He releases His only Son to be cruelly crucified by others – at the same geographical location.

†

This is the context for the first mention of the word "worship". It preceded the Passover instructions (concerning the sacrifice of a perfect lamb by each family) by several hundred years.

The Hebrew word used here for "worship" is *shachah* and means 'to prostrate, to bow down (as to royalty), to pay homage, to do reverence, to worship, to do obeisance'!

Except where idolatrous worship is mentioned, the same word is used in every other reference to worship throughout the Old Testament.

4

Worship Under the Law

By the time God revealed the Law to His people through Moses, idolatry was rife among the nations, and even the Israelites were engaging in idolatrous worship and following the religious practices of other nations.

The Law – widely understood to mean the Ten Commandments, although it encompassed far more than that – revealed God's blueprint for the lives of His people in terms of their personal lives, their relationships and their religious obligations.

Note: Our English word 'law' here is misleading, as what Moses received was not a legal document. The original meaning is closer to 'instruction' or 'teaching', and carries a sense of instructing students in a classroom.

So God gave the Law to address Israel's failings – personal, corporate and religious. The issues it addressed were not hypothetical or theoretical; they were real, current, urgent and obviously of great importance to God – to a God Who valued an ongoing relationship with His people.

†

Given the wide scope of the problems addressed by the Law, what would be the most important issue on God's mind? Should He deal with the sins of murder, dishonesty, adultery or greed? What part of human behaviour would be of the greatest concern to Him?

Where would He start?

The first law addresses idolatry, the worship of other gods: "No other gods before Me, no bowing down to idols or images" [See Ex.20:3-5].

So from God's perspective, the issue of true worship versus idolatry is at the very foundation of human life, and was His primary concern for the people's wellbeing.

In passing, it is interesting to note why God forbad the intermarriage of His people with those of other tribes: He knew that the Israelites would be tempted to follow their idolatrous ways and worship other gods [Deut.7:1-5].

†

The Law goes on to deal with many other aspects of life, but the amount of detail recorded concerning the issue of worship / idolatry is vast and completely overshadows the coverage of other issues. This alone should alert us to the importance of true worship.

Whilst the Law stressed the importance of the people's worship, we should note that it also regulated the people's daily lives. It would not have been sufficient for them to comply with the worship-versus-idolatry instructions without also living lives which honoured God. God-honouring lives and God-honouring worship: the two are related but also distinct, and God intended them to be complimentary.

Holy lives do not replace God-focussed worship, and engaging in true worship does not dispense with a godly lifestyle.

†

To better understand worship under the Law, we need to rewind to a time before God gave the Law, to the time when God's people were slaves in Egypt and were prevented from worshipping God, even if they wished to.

Eventually, God issued a challenge to Pharoah through Moses. The challenge was, *"Let My people go, that they may serve Me"* [Ex.8:1]. Just what did God mean by that? What kind of 'service' did He have in mind? What did He want from His people that they could not do in captivity?

The wording is clear: their release from Egypt was not primarily about their status as slaves, nor their suffering from being overworked. Although God was not unmindful of their plight, His challenge to Pharoah concerned the freedom of His people to *"serve"* Him.

Their release was not to facilitate a better lifestyle, nor to escape merciless taskmasters; it was to enable them to serve God away from a country where other gods were being served.

In Search of Worship

In all probability, they were 'serving' other gods by building structures for the Egyptians to worship idols. They were bound by another allegiance – both physically and spiritually.

Serving God

If you had not read the ongoing story in the book of Exodus, exactly how would you have expected the people to respond to God's *"serve Me"* challenge, once they escaped into the wilderness?

How can you serve God in a desert? What could you do? Whom could you help? To whom could you 'witness'?

The clue is in the word *"serve"*, which also translates as *"hold a feast to Me"* [Ex.5:1], *"sacrifice to Me"* [Ex.5:3] or, by implication, "worship Me". It means 'to be in bondage to', 'to have exclusive allegiance to', 'to minister to', 'to pay homage to', 'to wait upon'.

God's people were being called out of bondage in Egypt into a different bondage – a wholehearted allegiance to God which focussed their energies on ministering to Him, and acknowledged no other lord and master.

In every case where the word *"serve"* is used in this narrative, it describes a 'vertical' human response toward God and not 'horizonal' activities carried out on His behalf.

This is an important distinction.

†

Many other Scriptures make this clear, using the same word:

- *"Our livestock also shall go with us ... for of them must we take to serve the Lord"* [Ex.10.26]. The meaning is clear: they would select animals from their livestock to offer as sacrifices to the Lord, as part of their worship.

- *"Serve the Lord with gladness; Come before His presence with singing"* [Ps.100:2, NKJV].

There is a common misunderstanding which relates to this last verse (and similar verses).

21

To give a personal example, I had grown up with this verse, and to me its meaning was clear: do what you do with the right spirit, keep smiling and try not to feel resentful when too much is asked of you! Anyone who has been involved in Christian ministry will understand that occasionally there is the need to 'go the extra mile', and at such times I would remind myself to *"serve the Lord with gladness"* and try to minimise the internal gritting of teeth! Maybe you too have been there.

But the psalmist is not speaking about doing God's work without resentment; he is encouraging us to *worship the Lord* with joyful hearts – and goes on to inspire us to burst into song! I am ashamed to have got it wrong for so long!

- *"...You shall worship the Lord your God, and Him alone shall you serve"* [Matt.4.10].
- *"For this reason they are [now] before the throne of God and serve Him day and night"* [Rev.7:15]. If we understand that the primary, if not the only, activity of the saints in heaven is to worship God, serving Him before the throne must describe their worship, not their endless busyness running errands for Him!

In every case, the word *"serve"* describes human activities which are focussed on the Lord and directed to Him. Scripturally, then, serving describes man's vertical response to God, and not man's employment on earth, working on behalf of an absent boss!

This is not to say that the various 'Christian' activities which occupy many of us are invalid expressions of our love for God; they may well be the fruit of God-focussed lives and based on clear biblical directives, but we need to ask whether they are, of themselves, acts of worshipful ministering to the Lord or just horizontal expressions of our relationship with God.

Certainly, for God's people in the desert, the meaning was clear: "Minister to Me, wait on Me, pay homage to Me, worship Me alone, sacrifice to Me, hold a feast in celebration of Me."

†

Just as God's people were released from their bondage in Egypt to worship Him, and not just for their own comfort, we need to understand that our salvation is not primarily about the benefits we receive, but it releases us into a new 'bondage' – freeing us to 'serve' our new master. Our new freedom should enable us to focus our lives on 'serving' Him in homage and worship.

To put it another way, the goal of our salvation is far greater than a rescue plan for the good of mankind. It is a salvation *to* and not just a salvation *from*.

Moses' Tabernacle

Until this time, there had been no tangible location for God's presence on earth. Altars were built in various locations as people moved around. This changed when God revealed instructions for creating a mobile tabernacle which would accompany the people on their desert travels, and which would be the place for their worship.

In Exodus 25:8, God says, *"Let [the people] make Me a sanctuary, that I may dwell among them."* He gives Moses a blueprint for the construction of a tent, an ark, a mercy seat, a lampstand and many other things. The precise detail given is full of typology which has been successfully explored elsewhere and is well worth studying; the pattern of worship leaves nothing to chance or human imagination. There are instructions about clothing, oil, sacrifices and many other things. Skilled craftsmen carried out all God's instructions and eventually, two years after the Exodus [Ex.40:17], all is in place for tabernacle-based worship.

†

The worship involved sacrifices for sin, freewill offerings of various kinds and regular feasts of celebration. There were clear prohibitions as to what could and what could not be offered. Alongside what may seem to us to be heavy-duty regulations, there were also many promises which God made to the worshippers. These included regular rains, ample food supplies, good harvests, times of peace and success in battle. He promised that if the people would worship only Him, He would bless their food and water, remove sickness from them, prevent miscarriages and barrenness, and ensure their lives would not be cut short.

"You shall serve the Lord your God; He shall bless your bread and water, and I will take sickness from your midst. None shall lose her young by miscarriage or be barren in your land; I will fulfill the number of your days" [Ex.23:25-26].

Later on [Deut.28], Moses reminds the people of God's promises to bless every area of their lives if they live as He intended and worship only Him – but also adds a long list of curses which would result from disobedience, clearly stating:

"All these curses shall come upon you ... because you do not obey the voice of the Lord ... They shall be upon you as a sign [of warning to other nations] and for a wonder, and upon your descendants forever. <u>Because</u> you did not <u>serve</u> the Lord your God with joyfulness of ... heart [in gratitude] for the abundance of all [with which He had blessed you]" [Deut.28:45-47, emphasis added].

Far from saying they had not been busy enough working for Him, the serving mentioned here relates to their lack of God-fearing worship!

How different Israel's history would have been if they had served only God and avoided idolatry! Would similar blessings be available today for those who make God the focus of their worship?

The Ark – Symbol of God's Presence

Moses eventually hands over the leadership to Joshua, and the people journey on, still focussing their worship on the mobile tabernacle. God frequently renews His instruction about worshipping only Him, and the people frequently transgress and turn to idols.

The Scriptures record a recurring pattern of divine judgement and sometimes national repentance, and eventually the tabernacle finishes up at Gibeon, where its prominence seems to diminish [1Chr.21:29] – especially after the ark of the covenant (as it came to be called) was captured by the Philistines and placed in the temple of Dagon, the Philistine god.

This sacred symbol of God's presence caused havoc in the heathen temple, however, and also among the local population, so that the town's leaders decided to get rid of it.

They sent it to Gath, where it had a similar effect on the people, who then sent it on to Ekron, where it caused panic and the local people demanded its removal from their town!

†

In Search of Worship

Eventually (read the full story in 1 Samuel 6; 7 and 2 Samuel 6), after nearly a hundred years, the ark finished up in Obed-edom's house. With the ark absent, Israel's worship had reached a low point – but its presence in Obed-edom's house brought tangible blessings.

When David finally became king, his first priority was to recover the ark of God, which had been in foreign hands for so long. He missed the physical evidence of God's presence and all that the ark signified, and made its recovery his priority. What an example to set for his people! We might imagine how wonderful it would be if church leaders always sought the presence of God as their first priority. Obed-edom's experience might then follow.

The Ark was returned amid great celebration, during which King David danced before the Lord in exuberant worship and without inhibitions. 2 Chronicles 15:25-29 and 2 Samuel 6:5-15 describe the event. Singers were appointed (accompanied by harps, lyres, cymbals, cornets and trumpets), and they were to lead the procession as the ark was returned with great joy.

Only one person seems to have lost the plot: David's wife, who stayed indoors and despised her husband for his wild dancing before the Lord. She was obviously not rejoicing about the return of the ark, and David's wholehearted worship offended her. As a consequence she remained barren for the rest of her life.

This is a sobering thought for anyone who sidelines times of worship or despises those whose love for God is more important than personal decorum!

5

David's Tabernacle

The tabernacle which Moses set up in the wilderness is described in great detail – many chapters are devoted to its size, construction and furnishings.

Even the temple which was built later by Solomon is not described in such detail, although it was built with the finest materials and much gold.

In stark contrast to both of the above structures, the actual construction of David's tabernacle is not even mentioned [1Chr.15:1; 2Sam.6:17], and it is described only as *"a tent"*.

In fact, David laments to the prophet Nathan that the ark of the covenant *"remains under tent curtains"* [1Chr.17:1] while he himself lives in a permanent house. God's glory is never far from David's mind, and he is embarrassed by the contrast between his own luxurious dwelling place and the tent which houses the ark – the symbol of God's presence.

†

Is it strange, therefore, that this simple tent gets a mention many years later? The prophet Amos, speaking about God's future dealings with Israel, quotes God as saying, *"In that day, I will raise up the tabernacle of David, the fallen ... booth, and close up its breaches"* [Am.9:11].

The apostle James, during a debate about God's inclusion of the Gentiles in His plan of salvation, speaks to the other apostles and elders, and quotes the Amos scripture: *"After this I will come back and will rebuild the house [tabernacle] of David, which has fallen; ... I will set it up again, So that the rest of men may seek the Lord, and all the Gentiles"* [Acts.15:16-17].

But why?

What characterised David's tabernacle to make it special to God?

Obviously not the fabric, as animal skins would not have lasted for ever, and David had in mind to construct a more permanent home for the ark.

Neither was it designed to be a mobile sanctuary like Moses' tabernacle; it was erected in Jerusalem with no plans to go on tour around the country, so the simple construction was not about mobility.

If not the fabric, was it more about what it symbolised, what it represented and how it was used?

I think David's focus was on what it would contain, the symbolic presence of Almighty God, and not on its temporary covering.

He was so excited about the ark's return that he seems to have thought little about a glorious location for it once it arrived. There is surely something to be learned here: we should be focussed more on ushering in the presence of God than on the visible glory of its location.

†

David's preparations for the ark's return are interesting, and are recorded in 1 Chronicles 15.

- He summons all the priests, Levites and *"all Israel"* to Jerusalem for the big event.
- The priests and Levites had to *"sanctify"* themselves in readiness for carrying the ark.
- The ark had to be carried correctly – by the priests and Levites, and not on an ox cart.

(You may remember that the Philistines had used a cart to get rid of it, and also that David used a cart when bringing it from Abinadab's house to Jerusalem after its hundred year absence – with disastrous consequences for Uzzah who touched the ark during the journey. The Ark then spent three months in the house of Obed-edom where it brought noticeable blessing to Obed and everything he owned! When David heard about this, his fear subsided and he made plans to bring the ark back to Jerusalem.)

- The Levites were told to appoint singers and musicians from their ranks – to play and sing joyfully as the ark was returned.

There is significant detail about the instruments, who should play them, and how they should be played. David appointed trumpeters to precede the ark on its journey, announcing its arrival. Gatekeepers were appointed – presumably to ensure no-one else touched or approached the ark.

The whole company, numbering several thousand, set off with much noise and excitement.

When they arrived back at Jerusalem with the ark, it would be safe to say that everyone's attention was on the ark and all that it symbolised, and not on the simple tent into which it would be placed (except, of course, David's wife, as we saw earlier!)

So What was Unique About David's Tabernacle?

- It was not ornate or visibly striking.

God seems to value the ordinary! There was once a dirty stable where a special baby was born! There were also uneducated fishermen who became world-class evangelists! And of course, there was a shepherd who became a powerful king!

- It had no heavy curtain separating ordinary people from God's presence.

It was one space – no courtyard, no gates, no holy place and no holy of holies. It was accessible in a way not seen before, and surely indicated that God wanted, once more, to be intimate with His people. This may be surprising, given the fate of someone who actually died as a result of touching the ark, but it was still protected by gatekeepers and accessed only by the priests.

- The tabernacle was to be surrounded by quality music, and David issued more instructions about this than Moses did in relation to his more ornate tabernacle.

David, the musician and worshipper, wanted to ensure that the tabernacle was surrounded by praise and thanksgiving every day, and he appointed (and the record actually names them) skilled musicians to ensure that this happened. When you think of the myriads of music-makers throughout history, very few of their names have been preserved, especially for thousands of years, yet God considered the identity of

David's skilled musicians worth recording. They were, of course, primarily worshippers, not just skilled music-makers!

Their appointment was not an afterthought; David issued specific instructions about the music before the ark was recovered. All this detail about the music – and so little detail about the ark's resting place! David's priorities are clear – and an example to us all.

- This tabernacle seems to have been predominantly a place of joy and thanksgiving, possibly in contrast to the earlier rituals of Moses' tabernacle, where the emphasis was often on sin offerings and getting right with God.

Maybe it was unique in other ways, but clearly it pleased God, and He was content to identify with this simple structure, and promised to rebuild it in some way.

In every sense, He was the centre of the people's worship, and visitors came to honour Him and not just to admire an impressive building! I think He is still happy to identify with those who share that priority!

Centuries later there were many people who expected the Messiah to arrive in great power and glory, and who found it hard to accept that the greatest revelation of God showed up in a stable, worked in a carpenter's shop and rode on a donkey. As the Apostle John wrote, the Son of God became flesh and *"tabernacled ... among us"* [Jn.1:14]. His very name meant *"God with us"* [Matt.1:23] – Emmanuel.

David's tabernacle surely prefigured the revelation of Jesus, Who was truly God with us.

6

David – The Shepherd Who Became King

It is worth taking a closer look at this amazing character, about whom the Scriptures speak at length.

In fact, he is mentioned in over twenty-five books of the Bible, in both Testaments, and is of course listed in the genealogy of Christ himself.

David – the shepherd, the musician, the fearless warrior, the army commander, the outcast, the lover, the fugitive, the king, the adulterer, the father, the murderer – the list could go on.

Although he is a key biblical figure, David's life is not air-brushed to exclude his challenges and failings, and God was happy to include the full story in His 'book' for subsequent generations to read!

If ever there were a challenge to set out a profile of an ideal worshipper, surely David's track record would automatically disqualify him. Or so we might think. (We would do well to avoid making similar disqualifications when judging the worthiness of others who aspire to worship but have imperfect track records – which, of course, we all do.)

But for all his failings, inconsistencies and sins, David is spoken of by God Himself: *"I have found David son of Jesse a man after My own heart, who will do all My will…"* The prophet Samuel and the Apostle Paul both mention this divine affirmation [1Sam.13:14; Acts.13:22]. Despite his failings, something in David merited God's special attention.

About no other biblical character does God use the phrase *"a man after My own heart"*.

- God does not use this phrase about Job for his outstanding righteousness and integrity in the face of unbelievable tragedy.

- Nor Abraham, whom God called His friend.
- Nor Moses, the leader whom God chose as the faithful communicator of the Law.
- Nor Solomon, for all His God-given wisdom.
- Nor Enoch, who is recorded as having *"walked with God"* [Gen.5:24, NKJV].
- Not even the apostle John, the disciple whom Jesus loved.

Would this have anything to do with the fact that David was above all things a worshipper, who prioritised seeking God's presence?

Perhaps beyond any other biblical character, David shows us that God values what is in our hearts more than our usually imperfect behaviour! He is a worshipper *par excellence* and his life story should encourage us all.

†

The youngest of eight sons, David was a fine-looking lad with beautiful eyes but, in his father's eyes, was not destined for greatness. Jesse presented his seven elder sons to the prophet Samuel as potential candidates for a special anointing, but omitted to include David who was young, only a shepherd and evidently an afterthought! So David missed out when Samuel arrived and consecrated Jesse and the other sons. No doubt he took some flak from his older brothers after Samuel rejected them and then anointed him – the teenager whose only credentials involved looking after sheep!

From that moment, however, the Spirit of the Lord came mightily on David [1Sam.16].

His life story is an interesting one, and does not follow the usual path of those destined for royal duties. But through all his traumas, battles, rejection and suffering, he seems to have retained a confidence that his life was in God's hands and that God was always worthy of praise.

Perhaps the Psalms would not be so rich and meaningful if David had lived a simple life. Perhaps his struggles were actually responsible for the wealth of writings and songs which have encouraged so many for hundreds of years.

Above all the biblical characters, David was consistently a worshipper. He had a profound yet simple relationship with his God – a God to Whom he regularly prayed and Whom he regularly worshipped.

As a shepherd minding his flocks out in the hills, he must have spent hours making music and singing to his Maker. In fact, we can wonder whether any other occupation would have given him the time to compose so many songs. It is interesting that he first came to King Saul's attention as a skilled musician – not as a reliable shepherd! Saul, who would no doubt have had skilled courtiers to entertain him with soothing music, actually asked for David to play when troubled by an evil spirit. Knowing how the enemy hates worshipful music, we can draw our own conclusions about what David was playing!

It is in many ways remarkable that David, who lived about a thousand years before Christ, should feature so prominently in history, be included in the genealogy of Jesus, and have left a rich legacy of psalms and songs which are still known and loved.

David's Worship Preparations

Embarrassed by the fact that he lived in a comfortable house while God's 'residence' was merely a tent, David purposed to build God a permanent house – until this was halted by a message from God via the prophet Nathan. God told David that because of his history of war and bloodshed [1Chr.22:8], his son Solomon would be the one to build God a more permanent house. Because Solomon was still young, David decided to start making preparations, ready for Solomon when he grew up.

He drew up plans for the temple, and amassed vast quantities of stone, cedar wood, bronze, iron, silver, gold and precious stones in readiness for the time his son Solomon could take on the oversight of this important building.

Only the best materials were to be used, and this principle extended to the appointment of key people to minister in the temple. Many are named in the record – officers, judges, gatekeepers, priests, Levites, and, of particular interest to us, David appointed four thousand *"to praise the Lord with the instruments which I made for praise"* [1Chr.23:5].

In Search of Worship

That is not a misprint! *Four thousand* appointed to offer praise! They were to minister to the Lord twenty-four hours a day, in shifts, and it was their primary, if not their only, task.

In 1Chr.25 we have lists of those David appointed. Some were to prophesy with lyres, harps and cymbals. Others were specially trained in songs (note) *to* the Lord [1Chr.25:7], and they were all talented singers.

The importance David attached to providing the best for God's residence is beyond dispute. The quality of David's preparations and appointments is clear. Everything had to be of the highest order to reflect the greatness and glory of the Lord. And the appointment of singers and musicians was not an afterthought; they were appointed before the building work began and reflects David's determination that God should be praised at all times by skilled worshippers. What an example for us today!

†

I recently heard the music director of one of our great cathedrals being interviewed, in which he spoke in glowing terms about the commitment of his choristers, the quality of their voices, their training, the range of sacred music they performed and the purity of the sound they produced. This is all good – but I was left thinking about what was *not* said in the course of quite a lengthy interview. There seemed to be no awareness that the music should be for the glory of God, and that it was not an entity in and of itself. The focus was on producing excellent musical offerings (which no one would dispute), but there was no sense that the motivation was the glory of God. I love high quality music, but the interview left me feeling sad – almost sad on God's behalf that His glory was not central to the performance of the music.

†

It does seem comparatively rare to find the combination of high quality music and musicians along with a clear focus on seeking only God's glory. David got it right, in terms of his focus on God's glory and also the quality of his musicians.

Of course, acceptable worship comes from a heart of love and not necessarily from the performance of a skilled musician or suitable music. That is to say, an unskilled offering from a heart of love is probably far more acceptable to God than a flawless offering made from duty or habit.

God sees our hearts. But our aim should always be to produce the best we can with the skills we have – and always for His glory, not for ours.

7

The Key of David

"These are the words of the Holy One, the True One, He Who has the key of David, Who opens and no man shuts, and shuts and no one shall open" [Rev.3.7].

What does this mean? The risen Lord is speaking to the church in Philadelphia through the Apostle John while he is in exile on the island of Patmos. The Lord goes on to say that He has set before the church a door which is wide open – a door which no one is able to shut.

But what is the key of David? Why is David mentioned in this context?

The same phrase is found in Isaiah's prophecy [Is.22:22] where God says He will replace a corrupt official with a servant of His own choice – a man called Eliakim – to whom will be given all the authority he needs to be a father to the inhabitants of Jerusalem. God says He will lay upon his shoulder the key of David.

Commentators have suggested various interpretations, but there seems to be no general consensus as to what is meant. Could it mean that the Philadelphian church was being encouraged to move forward and evangelise? This seems unlikely as it would have little relevance to David. Could it refer to the dynasty of David, from whom came the Messiah? This also seems to make little sense. And in any case, the risen Lord is saying that *He* holds the key, even though in the Isaiah passage the key is to be given to the incoming ruler. The Philadelphian church is not being *given* the key; the key remains in the possession of the Lord, Who has apparently used it for their benefit.

†

Keys usually fit locks, and locks are usually to be found on gates or doors.

They have two purposes – to *protect from* or to *provide access to*.

In this case, the door, having been opened by the key of David, is wide open, and the implication is that the Philadelphian church should enter without hesitation!

So we can ask the question, was there a specific situation in which David had the key to lock or to unlock? Did David do something which sets him apart from every other biblical character?

I suggest there are several possible situations in which David's actions were unique:

- His first priority on becoming king was to retrieve the ark of the covenant – the symbolic evidence of God's presence which had been absent. That tells us that he valued 'God with us' more than 'God helping us'. His priority was not taking territory by military means, or having wealth or status; he wanted God's presence more than anything and made it his priority.

- David was the only king who succeeded in subduing the Jebusites who controlled the hill of Zion, which, interestingly, was located at the territorial junction of two tribes – the tribe of Benjamin, representing warfare, and Judah, the tribe of praise. Zion proved to be a key place in Israel's history and became the focus of the nation's worship. It also features prominently in God's eternal masterplan. The Psalms speak of the people's regular journeys up to this holy place to worship [Ps.120-134].

- David was unique in orchestrating the elaborate worship resources for the temple. No other individual, prophet or monarch has matched David's determination to honour God with such lavish worship. His whole life was a journey of worship which culminated in his preparation for twenty-four-hour worship in the temple. No other biblical character has come close to David's zeal and extravagance in providing for such awesome worship – and it is probably true that nothing has equalled it in modern times.

Taken together, could these 'key' accomplishments be identified as David's key? Certainly, he unlocked what had previously been locked – releasing the ark from captivity, establishing Zion as the centre of worship and, later on, opening the door for exuberant praise to ascend into heaven by appointing so many skilled musicians to oversee the temple worship. From a divine perspective, these acts might well be

In Search of Worship

considered the most significant achievements in his life – and we can add to this the fact that God promises to rebuild *"the tabernacle of David"* [Am.9:11].

†

If these aspects of David's life and achievements do help us to understand 'the key of David', we can ask what relevance they might have had to a struggling New Testament church. We can assume that the reference would have been understood by the leaders of the church, even if its application is less obvious to us.

David's priority in recovering the ark of God's presence may well have been 'key' to a church which, although busy with works and activities [Rev.3.8], had been struggling to uphold the truth and apparently lacked power. Were they being encouraged to prioritise seeking God's presence as the source of their strength?

David's second priority was the conquest of Zion – defeating and evicting the Jebusite squatters from God's holy mountain – the place from which corporate worship would ascend. Were the Philadelphian believers being encouraged to prioritise worship in the place where, apparently, Satan had established a synagogue?

And, finally, were they being encouraged to learn from David's example of orchestrating lavish worship for the glory of God?

Even if the Philadelphians understood the letter to have different and specific applications to their local situation, these 'key' aspects of his David's life can certainly teach us something of God's priorities today.

8

The Psalms

Of all the books in our Bible, the Psalms have inspired worship for many centuries.

Other books deal with the history of God's people, contain the wisdom of wise men, record the prophecies of God's messengers, and chronicle the life and ministry of Jesus while on earth. There are books of poetry, letters to individuals, doctrinal discourses, and some books which give us glimpses into the end times and God's eternal purposes.

But in the Psalms, we have a record of the personal expressions of individuals who depend on God for their wellbeing. And they express a wide range of human emotions – from anger and frustration, to confidence in God and praise for His provision and protection. There are prayers, there are testimonies and there are declarations of love for the Lord.

The Psalms are not all David's compositions, but many are, and many were intended to be sung. Some commentators suggest that some were set to Philistine or Hittite melodies – which might be of interest to those who object to Christians using 'worldly' tunes!

We can imagine David strumming his lyre whilst watching over his sheep, singing praise to God and enjoying His creation.

Many of the psalms encourage us to *"sing to the Lord"* [e.g. Ps.96:1] and singing to God was undoubtedly David's regular practice. Other psalms were written by Asaph. Many have no recorded author. Some are addressed *"to the Chief Musician"* [e.g. Ps.84:1].

†

Psalm 84 is one of my personal favourites.

In Search of Worship

It was written by the sons of Korah – which is interesting in itself, because their father had tried to start a rebellion against Moses [Num.16] and suffered an untimely death, together with all those who supported him. The earth opened and swallowed them up, as evidence of God's judgement on those who were challenging Moses' God-given authority. Even though his sons were not part of the conspiracy and did not die with him [Num.26:11], Korah's death must have encouraged them to stay faithful to God, and several of the psalms are attributed to them or their families.

Psalm 84 is a song. It is addressed to the Lord. In it the psalmist expresses a deep longing to be back in God's house. He is homesick for the courts of the Lord. He envies those who *"dwell in Your house"* [v.4] and have the honour of singing God's praises all day long.

He envies the birds who have unlimited access to the sanctuary and have even built their nests there. He says he would prefer to spend one day there as a doorkeeper (not even going in, but probably keeping guard at the entrance), rather than spend a thousand days living at ease with unbelievers.

Then he speaks about those "in whose heart are the highways to Zion" [v.5].

The language is reminiscent of the Songs of Ascents [Ps.120-134], where the psalmist traces the journey of pilgrims travelling up to the temple to worship from all parts of the country – where all the roads lead to Zion, much like the early motorways in the UK which all led to London.

The psalmist is saying that it is possible to have 'spiritual highways' in our hearts – various routes which have a common destination, which is God's residence and the centre of our worship.

There can be many catalysts which initiate our spiritual journeys into times of worship: fresh scriptural insights, conversations with other would-be travellers, revelations, outbursts of thanksgiving, answers to prayer and a fresh awareness of God's protection and provision, etc. The starting points for each worship journey may vary, but whatever stirs our hearts in the direction of 'Zion' (representing God's presence) will take us down one of those highways into His presence. I find that exciting – and encouraging.

The psalmist also states that those who make these journeys will be blessed, saying that strength increases as they near their destination. So in the process of travelling along one of those spiritual highways in pursuit of God's presence, we will *"go from strength to strength"* [v.7]. Now there's a thought! There are various ways of attempting to increase our spiritual maturity and strength, but we may overlook the possibility that it happens as a by-product of pursuing worship!

The psalmist also imagines that some of those highways may pass through dark valleys of sadness, but says that even they can be turned into places of blessing and fruitfulness.

When our hearts are focussed on worshipping the Lord and being in His presence, our journeys will be blessed and He will be our sun and shield – our guide and our protection.

Many other psalms speak about worship, but Psalm 84 expresses so much of the joy of making His presence our goal. For the pilgrims travelling up to Jerusalem, it happened only three times a year, but for us, by His grace, the invitation to *"draw near"* [Heb.4:16] is unlimited.

I love the concept of our hearts containing multiple highways, any of which can lead us into the presence of God and intimate worship.

†

More than any other book, the Psalms reverberate with expressions of praise and worship.

The Psalms also show us that there are many practical ways to express worship:

Here are a few:

- kiss the Son [Ps.2:12];
- sing to Him – the most frequently mentioned [Ps.5:11];
- shout for joy [Ps.5:11];
- be in high spirits [Ps.9:2];
- bow down before Him [Ps.22:27];
- meditate on His beauty [Ps.27:4];
- play the lyre and harp [Ps.33:2];

In Search of Worship

- clap your hands [Ps.47:1];
- shout to God [Ps.47:1];
- make a joyful noise [Ps.66:1];
- sound the timbrels [Ps.81:2];
- blow the trumpet [Ps.81:3];
- lift your hands [Ps.134:2];
- sing new songs to Him [Ps.149:1];
- play the tambourine [Ps.150:4];
- dance before Him [Ps.150:4];
- play the wind instruments [Ps.150:4];
- play the loud crashing cymbals [Ps.150:5].

Take your pick!

It seems that whatever instruments were to hand, the psalmist could employ them in praise and worship, not hesitating to bow down, clap his hands, dance, shout and (the most mentioned) sing praises to his Maker.

The reoccurring emotion is joy. God is great and many of the psalms are responses to His greatness. They encourage us to "Sing *to* Him", "Shout *to* Him", "Dance *to* Him" etc. Many of the psalms were written by David, and it seems that whatever trials he was going through, it didn't take a lot to stimulate his expressions of praise and worship.

9

Other Old Testament Examples

We have highlighted several examples of worship and worshippers in the Old Testament, looking especially at David and the Psalms, but in fact the worship theme is constant throughout – in the times of the judges, the kings and the prophets.

Here are a few more :

- King Jehoshaphat understood the importance of worship when Israel was about to be attacked by a large consortium of enemies. One of the Levites prophesied that the Lord would deliver His people, and in response, Jehoshaphat *"bowed his head with his face to the ground, and all Judah and the inhabitants of Jerusalem fell down before the Lord, worshiping Him. ... he appointed singers to sing to the Lord and ... they went out before the army, saying, 'Give thanks to the Lord, for His mercy and loving-kindness endure forever!' And when they began to sing and to praise, the Lord set ambushments against [their enemies] ... and they were [self-] slaughtered"* [2.Chr.20:18,21-22].

- Samuel's parents (Hannah and Elkanah) worshipped the Lord on their annual visited to Shiloh, bringing sacrificial offerings [1Sam.1:4,19,28].

- One of the most striking examples concerns Shadrach, Meshach and Abednego, three high-ranking officials in King Nebuchadnezzar's Babylonian government. The narrative is also interesting because it highlights the use of music in worship: King Nebuchadnezzar made a decree that every man who heard the sound of the horn, pipe, lyre, trigon, harp, dulcimer or bagpipe, or any kind of music, should fall down and worship the golden image of himself [Dan.3:5]. The punishment for refusing to bow down was a visit to a very hot furnace! As servants of God, they refused, and were thrown into the furnace which had been heated up seven times hotter than usual. However, God protected them and they were subsequently honoured by the king, who then decreed that no-one should speak evil of the God Who had delivered these brave men who had refused to worship any other god. Not the result that the demonic plotters had hoped for!

- Another example concerns Daniel, who refused to obey a law which prevented anyone from praying to any god or man except the king [Dan.6:7]. God-fearing Daniel continued to get *"down upon his knees three times a day and prayed and gave thanks before His God"* [Dan.6:10]. His jealous colleagues got him thrown into the lions' den, much to the king's consternation. The result of Daniel's refusal to acknowledge any other god led to King Belshazzar making a decree that *"in all my dominion men must tremble and fear before the God of Daniel, for He is the living God ... and His kingdom shall not be destroyed"* [Dan.6:26]. Again, not the outcome that Daniel's jealous colleagues had hoped for, but one which exalted the fame of the One and Only True God!

- When the exiles returned to Jerusalem from Babylon they should have started to rebuild the temple, but they were discouraged and concentrated on building their own homes instead [Hag.1]. Through the prophet Haggai, God challenged them to prioritise the work of rebuilding the temple so that He could again be resident among them and also bless them. They had not made this their priority and consequently had not been blessed with good harvests and fulfilling lifestyles [vs.6-11]. God promised that the result of seeking His presence would bring them much blessing, and amazingly, they repented and worshipped the Lord. In response, God said through His prophet, *"I am with You"* [Hag.1:13]. Their failure to prioritise worship led to practical problems (this is worth noting) and their change of heart released God's blessings upon every area of their lives.

God's people repeatedly fell into idolatry, and His messengers constantly tried to encourage their repentance and return to true worship. The reoccurring theme is one of worship versus idolatry.

10

Worship in the New Testament

Some people have wondered why, compared to the lengthy instructions God communicated to Moses about Israel's worship in the Old Testament, there is little about worship in the Gospels and other New Testament books – or so it seems.

If we examine the references which do appear, however, we get a sense that it continued to be important. Whilst few instructions are recorded, there are many examples of individuals to whom worship was important.

- The wise men.

In the New Testament, the first mentioned worshippers were the wise men who came to visit the baby Jesus. The word used here (*proskuneo*) means 'to kiss, to prostrate oneself in homage, to adore'.

They were astrologers who had received a divine revelation that a king had been born. They knew that he was *"born King of the Jews"*, and the record states that they came *"to worship Him"* [Matt.2:2]. (Surely not – they were neither Jews nor Christians! This shows that a divine revelation can be received even by those who are not believers.) That is, the one purpose of their visit was to pay him homage and to fall down before him in worship. They were not ambassadors representing others; they were not seeking recognition for themselves or their country. They had one purpose: to find the newborn king of a country which was not theirs and to worship him. Amazing!

Their gifts were significant too and very costly. No popping into the local supermarket for a quick box of chocolates! What a story! They were the first, and very probably the only, worshippers to welcome the Son of God on earth. (It is true that the shepherds also came, got very excited and praised God as they returned to their flocks and shared the good news with others, but, perhaps strangely, there is no record of them worshipping the baby Jesus.)

In Search of Worship

The word *proskuneo* is consistently used throughout the New Testament, including in the book of Revelation. The fact that John, the writer of Revelation, uses the same word to describe what he saw of heavenly worship suggests that our worship on earth is not something peculiar to our age, but just a foretaste of what we will continue to do when we reach heaven. Best get in some practice while we can!

- Jesus' wilderness encounter.

As previously noted, Satan's main purpose in tempting Jesus was to divert His worship away from His Father and onto Satan himself. Undoubtedly, the temptations to ease His hunger, to miraculously fly from the pinnacle of the temple and to gain control of all the kingdoms of the world were real enough, but the climax of the temptations focussed on satanic worship versus true worship. Satan had no higher purpose than to achieve this – and his present activities have a similar goal: to prevent or divert our worship of God.

- Jesus' conversation with the Pharisees.

When speaking to the Pharisees, Jesus reiterated the importance of the first commandment – to worship only God.

- Jesus speaking to the Samaritan woman.

A Samaritan woman discusses worship with Jesus when they meet at a village well. She is concerned about where it should happen, but Jesus explains to her in remarkably direct terms that true worship is a matter of spirit and truth, and not location.

He also says that His Father is *"actively seeking"* those who will worship Him *"in spirit and truth"* [Jn.4:23, NCV] – surely implying that worship would spring from the hearts of believers and not be restricted to a specific location.

There is no other scriptural reference to God the Father *"actively seeking"* anything else! (As it says in the Psalms, *selah*, or in modern English, wow!)

This revelation is profound, and is especially surprising because Jesus was speaking to a non-Jew, to a woman and not even to one of His followers. It was a key revelation that true worship did not depend on a temple building or special location. Is there also a hint here that worship *"in spirit and truth"* could (and would) reach beyond the limitations of being a Jew?

Jesus Himself continued to visit the temple, but His perfect understanding of true worship was not confined to a specific building.

- Jesus in the temple.

That the temple continued to be the focus of Jewish worship is evident from the incident when Jesus, with righteous anger, turned out all the traders – men who were making money from those who came to make worship offerings! Does this remind us of the time when Satan was expelled from heaven because of his merchandising [Ezek.28:16]? Clearly worship and making personal profit do not sit comfortably together.

- Temple worship continued.

The feasts [Ex.23] centred on the temple and were even attended by non-Jews. According to John 12, Greeks also travelled up to Jerusalem to join in.

Peter and John are recorded as going to the temple for the regular time of prayer and worship when they met a crippled man and healed him [Acts.3].

- An Ethiopian visitor.

A high-ranking Ethiopian court official travelled up to Jerusalem specifically to worship at the temple in Jerusalem [Acts.8].

- Paul the apostle.

The Apostle Paul says he continues to worship the same God his fathers worshipped [Acts.24].

- Lydia.

Lydia, who lived in Thyatira, was already a worshipper of God when Paul arrived on his missionary journey [Acts.16:14].

- Paul and Silas.

Paul and Silas were *"singing hymns of praise to God"* [Acts.16:25] whilst imprisoned for preaching about Jesus.

- Hebrews.

In Search of Worship

The book of Hebrews expounds the new freedom we have to worship because of Jesus' perfect sacrifice for sin, which replaced the old system of making regular worship offerings to God. We are encouraged to *"draw near"* [Heb.4:16; 10:22] to God in confidence and with boldness.

†

Throughout the New Testament, many people instinctively worshipped Jesus when they met Him: a leper, a local ruler, the disciples, a Canaanite woman, Mary of Magdala, a blind man, Titus Justus, to name just a few.

There are various indications that the early believers were worshippers. In Ephesians Paul says those who believe in Christ are destined to live *"for the praise of His glory"* [Eph.1:12].

He also speaks of believers being built into a holy temple – corporately to be a dwelling place for the Lord – and temples are essentially places of worship. Those of us who are believers have this responsibility – to be built together as a spiritual edifice, the primary function of which is to facilitate worship. Wow! How often does that sentiment appear in the mission statement of church groups?

In the list of ministries Paul gives to the Ephesians, God's purpose is clearly stated as building up the body of Christ (the church) – surely that we might be equipped to fulfil our calling as a holy temple for the offering of spiritual worship.

He also lists some practical instructions to the believers, including speaking out in *"psalms and hymns and spiritual songs ... and making melody with all your heart to the Lord"* [Eph.5:19].

†

We can see, therefore, that far from being absent from the New Testament records, worship continues to be central to the life of believers. In His wisdom, God knew that with the Holy Spirit's presence and inspiration, those who believed in His Son would instinctively find worship rising from their hearts without the need for long 'Levitical' chapters of detailed instructions!

In more recent times, there is evidence that when the church has experienced renewal or revival, this has released a new dimension of worship – often in music and song.

Conversely, in times of spiritual drought and unbelief, the flow of worship has dried up and the church has not produced a lasting legacy of worship.

At this present time it would be difficult to find a live and growing church which did not recognise the importance of corporate worship. We have seen churches die which have focussed on ministering to men and neglected to focus on ministering to God in worship.

As the Westminster Confession succinctly puts it, "The chief end of man is to glorify God and to enjoy him for ever."

Let us never allow horizontal ministries to replace our primary purpose of doing just that, for out of that will flow all kinds of God-breathed initiatives which will accomplish His purposes on earth. It was only when the disciples had worshipped the risen Jesus that He said to them, *"Go ... and make disciples of all the nations"* [Matt.28:19]. Likewise, it was only after Jesus had treble-checked Peter's love and devotion to Him that He commissioned him to, *"Feed My sheep"* [Jn.21:7].

Worship in Heaven

Heavenly worship is described several times in Revelation, the last book in the Bible, and it is interesting to note the forms it takes.

The four living creatures around God's throne continually offer *"glory and ... thanksgiving and honor"* [Rev.7:12], and the twenty-four elders respond by prostrating themselves before God and worshipping Him. They also sing and have musical instruments – singing a new song of praise to the Lamb, mentioning His worthiness, His sacrificial death and His redemptive purpose in making a kingdom of kings and priests. They also sing and have musical instruments [Rev.5.8]. Throughout the centuries angels have also been depicted in icons, frescos and paintings as having musical instruments; artists have always understood heaven to be alive with music – music focussed on praising God for Who He is and what He has done. The angels also have golden bowls containing the prayers of God's people, which they appear to be offering to God. In context, it seems unlikely that these are 'request' prayers; more likely, they are expressions of human praise and thanksgiving. John also saw every created being crying out together in praise and worship, and this inspires the elders to prostrate themselves in worship again. This seems to happen regularly.

Later, John saw the 144,000 standing on Mount Zion with the Lamb, singing a new song of worship. Others sang the song of Moses and the song of the Lamb – songs addressed to the Lord God [Rev.15]. And finally, in the new Jerusalem [Rev.22], His servants shall worship before His throne, and also see His face (i.e. they will be facing Him and not preoccupied with anything else!)

There are references to *"a new song"* [Rev.5:9], *"the song of the Lamb"* and *"the song of Moses"* [Rev.15:3]. So, could it be that earthly songs even find their way into the repertoire of heaven's musicians? If they do, they will have only one theme: the exaltation of the Godhead!

There will be no place for songs which educate us with doctrinal truth (God knows it all already) or songs that focus on our needs!

There will not even be songs which the heavenly beings sing to each other about God; according to the record in Revelation, the songs are addressed to God and sung to Him:

- the elders in 4:11;
- the cherubim and elders in 5:9;
- the angels, cherubim and elders in 5:13;
- the angels, cherubim and elders in 7:12;
- the elders in 11:17-18;
- those marked by God in 15:3-4;
- an angel in 16:5-6.

Heavenly worship is always God-facing, always directed to Him and always about His greatness and Christ's redemptive ministry.

So it seems that worship on earth and worship in heaven are not dissimilar – they have common themes, express themselves in physical ways, often involve song and musical instruments, and are always directed toward God. In heaven there is no higher activity. Maybe on earth the same should be true!

Once again, now is a good time to practise!

End-time Worship

Whilst we know from Scripture that God will be worshipped for ever and ever, as we have just seen from the book of Revelation, we are also given glimpses into the heavenly conflict of the end times, in which the issue of worship is central.

Revelation is a prophetic insight into the end times, as revealed to the apostle John on the island of Patmos. It offers glimpses into a realm we cannot see – the dwelling place of God, beyond time and space – and events largely beyond the comprehension of human understanding. Enough is revealed, however, to assure us that such a realm does exist, that humanity has a meaningful context beyond what is seen, and that God's purposes will ultimately triumph over every evil scheme of man and Satan.

The curtain of time is pulled back just enough for us to see that in eternity the worship of God will continue – in glorious Technicolor, combining angelic splendour with human devotion, and that it will always focus on God Himself. The apostle John attempts to describe in words what is beyond the power of human minds to comprehend, speaking of the glory and majesty of God, and of the perpetual worship of heavenly beings surrounding His throne.

In this prophetic book about the ultimate triumph of good over evil, when God is victorious over all His enemies we might expect the story to end with scenes of peace and of justice and eternal righteousness. And of course it does – but that is not all.

The conclusion, the goal, the climax and the fulfilment of the human story concerns the central issue of restored worship, where demonic attempts to divert worship away from God are thwarted. The end of the 'story' is not about control of new territory (as in many human conflicts), nor just about restoring peace on earth or establishing righteousness in place of injustice. Each of those things will take place, but the central issue, according to the book of Revelation, is that God alone will be worshipped.

It is worth looking in more detail about how this will take place and at the enemy's desperate schemes to prevent it happening. Even though God knows exactly how things will end, He will allow evil to take its course and will not override the consequences of man's freewill choices to pursue evil.

Whilst theologians may not agree about the sequence and time-scale of the events described in the book of Revelation, the language is graphic and the prophetic glimpses into this 'other world' convey a clear message about the conflict between a holy God and a demonic power determined to be worshipped.

After recording the letters to various churches, John describes in some detail what he saw of heavenly worship.

There are four living creatures who never stop saying, *"Holy, holy, holy, Lord God Almighty, Who was and is and is to come!"* [Rev.4:8] offering glory, honour and thanksgiving to God on His throne.

Their worship sparks off the worship of the twenty-four elders who fall prostrate in worship before God, throwing down their crowns before Him.

The four living creatures and the twenty-four elders join forces to worship the Lamb, singing a new song, and saying, *"You are worthy to take the scroll, And to open its seals"* [Rev.5:9].

Then John hears the voices of many angels ("ten thousand times ten thousand and thousands of thousands" [Rev.5:11]) joining in to worship the Lord: "Worthy ... is the Lamb that was sacrificed to receive power and riches and wisdom and might and honor and blessing" [Rev.5:12, AMP].

Then John hears every created thing in heaven and on earth, joining in to honour and worship the Lamb.

†

The record is sprinkled with other references to the ongoing worship in heaven, and to those who *"serve Him day and night in His sanctuary"* [Rev.7:15] – which, as we saw earlier, means they were engaged in worship, not running errands.

Later chapters record elements of the conflict between God and the devil, and God's judgements on those who refuse to abandon evil practices and continue to worship idols.

Even when angels were authorised to wipe out a third of mankind for their continued idolatry, worshipping demons and idols of gold and silver [Rev.9:20] – the people did not repent of their idolatrous worship and evil ways.

The End of Idolatry

The record describes Satan as a dragon [Rev.13], and the dragon gives his own power and authority to what is described as a beast – whose deadly wound is miraculously healed. The whole earth is amazed at this miracle and everyone falls down in homage to the beast and worships it, even though the beast is slandering God and blaspheming His name. Another beast enforces this idolatry, compelling everyone to pay homage to the original beast and worship it.

People also worship the dragon. Dare we say that Satan seems to value worship more than many of God's children!

Chapter 16 records various judgements against those who remain alive, but still they refuse to repent of their evil deeds and acknowledge God, blaspheming His name rather than admitting that He alone is worthy of their worship.

Satan is eventually bound and cast into the abyss, which is sealed above him, for a thousand years – after which he is released for a short time to lead a vast army against Jerusalem.

As they encircle Jerusalem, fire descends from heaven and consumes them, and the devil is then hurled into a fiery lake to join the beast and false prophet, to endure an eternity of torment.

After that, idolatry is finally crushed and God emerges as the only focus of worship for ever and ever.

Revelation 21 and 22 describe a holy city, a new Jerusalem, into which no evil will enter, and where God's throne will be established. He will be the centre of men's worship [Rev.22:3] and idolatry will cease to exist.

†

The prophet Zechariah speaks about this exciting time [Zech.14] when God destroys the demonically-led forces which make one final attempt to destroy Jerusalem. Zechariah's prophecy is particularly interesting in the context of our theme of worship. He says, *"And everyone who is left of all the nations which came against Jerusalem shall go up from year to year to worship the King, the Lord of hosts, to keep the Feast of Tabernacles ... And it shall be that whoso of the families of the earth shall not go up to Jerusalem and present themselves, upon them there shall be no rain"* [Zech.14:16-17].

And there will be a special judgement on the people of Egypt, if they refuse to go up: *"...upon them shall there be no rain, and there shall be the plague with which the Lord will smite the nations that go not up,"* which clearly references Egypt's refusal to let God's people go to worship Him in the desert centuries earlier.

Note that there is a link here between worship ascending to God and rain descending from heaven!

As it says in the Psalms, s*elah!*

†

So, this is where the story ends – or rather never ends! Satan's cosmic battle to be the focus of man's worship ends with his eternal judgement and confinement, but true worship continues because God is worthy of unending praise, in heaven and on earth.

11

The Songs We Sing

Having seen that much of heaven's worship seems to be expressed in song, it is worth considering what kinds of song get sung on earth – more specifically, what kind of songs many of us sing in the context of our church meetings.

It is of course erroneous to equate music with worship; they are not the same thing.

Worship does not depend on accompanying music.

Worship can be silent, spoken or expressed in movement and dance.

But there has always been a strong link between them. When John Newton discovered God's 'amazing grace' two hundred years ago, he wrote the now-famous hymn in which he anticipated "[singing] God's praise" for a thousand years and more.

†

The Psalms contain over sixty references to *"[singing] to the Lord"*, and it would be hard to find a church where singing did not feature in its meetings. So, whilst worship does not need to be expressed in music and song, it frequently, and historically, is! It is hard to imagine church meetings where, for example, the reading of poems replaces the singing of songs.

Long before the Christian era, the worship of God's people was often expressed in song. As the Christian church has developed over the centuries, new denominations have sprung up and produced their own hymnbooks to include the new hymns or songs which have flowed from the fresh revelations of the movement.

Methodism, for example, was born in song, and there is evidence that when Methodists were 'born again' they began to sing![4] It seems that new life easily spills over into musical expression and that this is quite natural.

John Wesley – obviously aware of this situation – set out some guidelines for the singing Methodists in which, after giving some helpful practical instructions, he writes:

"Above all, sing spiritually. Have an eye to God in every word you sing. Aim at pleasing Him more than yourself or any other creature. In order to do this, attend strictly to the sense of what you sing, and see that your heart is not carried away with the sound, but offered to God continually."[5]

Sound advice indeed!

†

Some of us have been around churches and hymn/song books for many years. We have seen most of them, sung from most of them, abstained from singing some of the songs and enjoyed singing others. We have sung with choirs, pipe organs, harmoniums, orchestras, pianos, guitars, drums; sung with no instruments, sung with too many instruments; sung in tune, sung out of tune; sung in chapels, high churches, low churches, schools, halls, forests, concert halls, fields and of course in the bath!

We have not always meant the words we have sung; we have not always *understood* the words we have sung! But of course the singing must go on – because we are Christians, we go to church and that's what people do in church!

I well remember singing the following song in Sunday School, aged around seven to eight years. Because it had a catchy tune, we sung it with great gusto... *but the words!* I've never found it in a hymn book, but the words went something like this:

---

[4] Preface to hymnbook *Christian Hymns;* Evangelical Movement of Wales (1977).
[5] Ibid.

"Sound the battle cry; see the foe is nigh;" followed by the chorus, "Rouse then soldiers; rally round the banner; ready, steady; pass the word along."

I don't remember having nightmares, but the thought of "nigh foes" might have been unnerving for an eight-year-old!

Also confusing for a churchgoing child were the words of a harvest hymn, which spoke of ploughing the fields and then scattering. I had impressions of farm workers working hard and then running for cover – an image which still makes me smile. It never occurred to me that the hymn's second line was needed to complete the picture.

I was also quite worried by the hymn 'All hail the power of Jesus' name', which spoke of angels' prostate falling (was it a disease, or like manna?) No-one bothered to explain to a young child that it referred to their posture (prostrate) and not their medical condition.

I also remember a meeting where the congregation was expected to sing 'O come all ye faithful' early in November – and, yes, the last verse was included, "Yea, Lord, we greet Thee, born this happy morning."

More recently I was in a morning service where the following hymn was sung: "The day Thou gave us, Lord, has ended; the darkness falls at Thy behest." No-one even batted an eyelid!

It seems that even as adults we can sometimes be afflicted by a brainless lethargy when it comes to singing hymns and songs in church. Do the angels tune in and have a good laugh?

†

But does it really matter what we sing?

If people enjoy singing 'Jerusalem', does it matter that its contents are totally fanciful and inaccurate, as long as people enjoy reaching the high notes and are having a good time?

(Not that 'Jerusalem' appears in most hymnbooks of course – but it does illustrate the fact that singing can be rewarding even when the words are not consciously understood or, at worst, nonsense!)

But in our present search for meaningful worship, it is valid to examine what and why we sing, as songs feature prominently in our worship.

So, What Do We Sing?

It has been interesting to review the content of dozens of hymn and song books, and to realise what a wide range of subjects they cover. Many hymns from earlier years are no longer sung, some more modern ones had their day but soon fall into disuse, but some survive and find their place in current worship. Some are boringly simple and some are too complicated for an average congregation to learn. Some are inspiring and some are, frankly, depressing!

Christian songs/hymns can be listed under several headings. The following list is not exhaustive, but gives a broad analysis of themes:

- There are those which are teaching aids, and expound doctrinal truths.

This was especially true of the songs of the Wesleys. Many of their hymns are full of profound truth and were educational. An example would be 'And can it be'.

- Some songs are essentially prayers.

Examples would be 'Abide with me' (how many people consciously realise they are petitioning the Almighty before the cup final kick-off?) and 'Guide me, O Thou great Jehovah'.

- Some are songs of testimony.

Life-changing experiences have often produced new songs, and these have added to the rich archive of Christian songs we have today. The problem comes when congregations are expected to sing such songs – songs which express other people's experiences but do not necessarily reflect their own! Examples would be 'I'm so happy, here's the reason why' and 'What a wonderful change in my life has been wrought.

- Songs of exhortation.

There are many songs which tell others what to do!

Examples: 'Come, let us sing for joy to the Lord', and 'Come, let us enter in'.

They have their place!

- Songs inviting sinners to repent.

The Victorians were good at these, and the assumption was that there were 'sinners' present in the meetings who needed to be invited/encouraged to respond to the offer of salvation.

In our culture they now seem sentimental and emotional, and it is hard to think of a context in which they would be appropriate.

Examples would be 'Where is my wandering boy tonight?' and 'Come home, come home' and 'Softly and tenderly Jesus is calling'.

- Scripture in song.

Many Scriptures have been set to music – often verbatim – including quite a few psalms.

Lyrics from two examples are "Thy word is a lamp unto my feet and a light unto my path" [Ps.119:105, KJV] and "Therefore the redeemed of the Lord shall return and come with singing unto Zion; and everlasting joy shall be upon their head" [Is.51:11, KJV].

For some people, this source of material for songs was highly prized, and in setting Scripture to music, you just couldn't go wrong. It is also true that some of our greatest composers have left a rich legacy of sung Scriptures, in such works as Handel's 'Messiah' and Mendelssohn's 'Elijah', although for obvious reasons these are not regularly used in church services!

- Songs of battle.

When the church has focussed on confronting the powers of darkness, or seen itself as a spiritual army, it has produced songs which reflect that military stance. Some denominations have a history of this aspect of church life. More recently, some groups have engaged in public demonstrations of strength which have produced songs with a military flavour.

Examples of this genre would be 'Stand up, stand up for Jesus', 'Onward Christian soldiers, marching as to war' and, more recently, 'In heavenly armour we'll enter the land'.

- Songs with mixed messages.

In Search of Worship

There are many! Some cover the whole spectrum of human life, some combine prayer with doctrinal explanation, some seem to have little to say, and some leave us confused as to what they are saying.

- Songs of celebration.

These are songs which celebrate God's character and provision – songs which we sing to each other about Him. Some examples are 'To God be the glory (great things he hath done)', 'My hope is built on nothing less', 'I will sing the wondrous story', or 'Come ye that love the Lord and let our joys be known'. Many of our songs and hymns fall into this category.

- Songs of praise and worship.

These are songs which are addressed to God, and express thanksgiving, praise and worship. You might be surprised to learn that these are a minority in most hymn/song books!

It is certainly an interesting exercise to identify the subject of the songs we sing and to ask for what purpose we are singing them at any particular time. Clearly, some songs have a particular relevance to specific situations, some can be age-related (differing genre and music styles), and some have a broader use than others. Some songs are best suited to performance by individuals, some require considerable practice and skill, and some are better suited to congregational use. Some need little musical accompaniment, whereas others would benefit from full-blooded orchestral support!

Then there is the whole area of the marriage of words and music – good words ruined by weak tunes, and stirring music linked to mediocre words. But that is a whole study in itself, and not our focus at present – although I am seriously tempted to list some notorious examples!

In summary then, how many of the hymns/songs we sing really qualify as worship songs?

What defines them in relation to other Christian music?

We saw that in many of the psalms, everything was directed *to* God, and not just said or sung *about* Him. Whether it was singing, shouting, dancing, playing instruments, clapping hands or bowing down – everything was centred on God.

†

Singing to each other is beneficial for us, and I'm sure God does not mind hearing us reminding ourselves of His love. In fact when God gave Moses instructions about the Law he was told to encourage families to rehearse everything God had done to his children. They were to speak to each other about God's goodness and provision, and there is a sense in which our songs can also instruct and remind us of all God has done. These songs have their place, but singing to each other *about* Him is not the same thing as singing *to* Him.

In a loving marriage relationship, we may tell another person how wonderful our spouse is, extolling his or her virtues and saying how much we love him or her. But if your spouse was standing beside you, and you ignored them whilst continuing to speak about them to the third party, they would probably be thinking, "I wish you could say all those lovely things *to* me and not just speak *about* me to other people as though I were not here!"

Singing to each other about the Lord accounts for a substantial proportion of our Christian repertoire. And many of those songs can actually be prayers or requests – genuine, meaningful and acceptable as they may be. But, by strict definition, do they actually constitute worship?

†

There are many songs which do qualify as songs of worship. Let's look together at an example of one such song which perfectly expresses true worship and which has led many into a meaningful place of worship.

It begins, "We are here to praise You, lift our hearts and sing."

So, why is this song a model?

- The song is addressed *to* God;
- it expresses our determination to bring the best we can bring;
- it recognises our relationship to God as our Father;
- it states our purpose as giving Him pleasure and delight;
- it springs from a heart of love and not duty or fear;
- it tells God that we love Him (not just telling others that we love Him!)

Such expressions of our love *to* Him (not just *for* Him) invariably open the door for His visitation!

Let's Be Honest

I grew up in a church environment where songs of personal testimony were sung regularly. We lustily sang songs with lyrics like, "What a wonderful change in my life has been wrought, since Jesus came into my heart" – but as a churchgoing lad with no dramatic history of rampant sinfulness, I often felt I had missed out on what I presumed everyone else had experienced! There were many such songs, and even then I was aware of being slightly hypocritical – or at least unspiritual – when expected to sing some of them!

Songs of personal testimony have their place, but if we expect everyone else to join in, we may be encouraging a degree of dishonesty! Other people's expressions of worship may well be wholehearted and honest, but sometimes our own experience may be different.

We may sing words like, "I give You all my life," or, "You mean everything to me," but whilst they may express our aspirations, we may not be being entirely honest! However, the Lord knows our hearts, and I'm sure He understands our aspirations even if they do not express our present reality. So whilst some hymns/songs may express our hope and genuine aspirations, I suggest it is worth an occasional 'reality check' in the interests of honesty – as God knows all about us anyway! We noted Wesley's wise words earlier: "Have an eye … of what you sing."

Even in this matter the enemy would love to bring us into condemnation: "You're a hypocrite. What you are singing is not true!" Nothing blocks the flow of worship like a dose of self-condemnation.

This is not to discourage us from bringing our offerings of praise, but rather to encourage us to ensure our songs focus more on His unchanging integrity than our dubious statements of intent!

12

What Happens When We Worship?

Have you ever wondered what actually happens when we worship? Have there been times when you've been tempted to think that moments of worship are unimportant or even a waste of time?

What follows may surprise you, but should be encouraging!

Here are some pointers:

- The Lord is exalted.

This is by far the most important!

For some reason, He loves us to draw near to Him in worship.

How do we know that?

The design of the tabernacle and the subsequent temple both demonstrate the fact that God loves to be among His people. The tent of meeting for Israel in the desert served the same purpose, when God's 'tent' travelled with the people. At that time, the sin issue prevented the people from having close contact with him, but He nevertheless made it clear that He was with them and not watching from afar.

Psalm 50.23 states: "He who brings an offering of praise and thanksgiving ... glorifies Me..."

Nowhere in Scripture does God refuse to acknowledge praise and worship.

For reasons which are beyond us, the worship he receives from angels does not satisfy His heart, and He delights in His children when they express their love for Him.

He is more than worthy of our praise and worship, and enjoys it.

- He inhabits our praises.

In Search of Worship

Psalm 22:3 says, *"...thou ... inhabitest the praises of Israel"* [KJV]. But is this an isolated sentiment – a passing observation of a romantic psalmist? Does God really 'inhabit' the praises of men? Is there any other indication in Scripture that supports this statement?

A powerful example of this principle is found in 2Chr.5, where Solomon dedicates the place of worship he has just built for God.

The musicians and singers had come together to offer praise to the Lord, and were joined by 120 priests blowing trumpets. The record states, *"And when the trumpeters and singers were joined in unison, making one sound to be heard in praising and thanking the Lord ... then the house of the Lord was filled with a cloud, So that the priests could not stand to minister because of the cloud, for the glory of the Lord filled the house of God"* [2Chr.5:13-14].

Wow! Not your average church service!

These were not wacky extremists! They were not even charismatics! They were ordinary priests trying to do what they had done many times, but the lavish offering of praise and worship attracted God's special presence and they were soon doing 'carpet time', as they say in some circles!

Similar things have been experienced more recently during sustained times of worship, and some of those present have been unable to stand, seemingly pressed to the floor by the Lord's overwhelming presence – evidence (if evidence is needed) that He inhabits our praises.

Whilst other scriptures indicate that God does inhabit specific places, it is worth mentioning that there are no other references to God inhabiting something that we *do.* He inhabits (the word means 'to live in, to settle down in, or dwell at ease') the praises of His people in a special way. Nowhere does it say that He inhabits our prayers, our preaching, our good works or any other religious activity.

Those who have experienced sustained times of praise and worship will know that there is indeed a special awareness of God's presence when He is the centre of our praise – sometimes almost a tangible presence of the Divine which can be felt and even smelt.

It is an awesome thing to be in the presence of an Almighty God Who loves to 'settle down', even if briefly, in the praises of His people. We can ask ourselves why this awesome experience is not at the top of our church (or personal) agendas!

- The perception of our problems can change.

Times without number, those who have chosen to worship the Lord have found that the difficulties they faced when they approached times of worship have either disappeared or been seen in a new context. Sometimes an eternal perspective changes everything, and worshippers find themselves no longer 'under the circumstances'!

- Personal holiness results.

When we hear that God says, *"...be holy, for I am holy"* [Lev.11:44], we may make every effort to be more holy, try harder and set out on a self-improvement programme, assuming that greater holiness results from tougher self-discipline. To a degree this may work! But we have found that personal holiness can be a by-product of our times of worship, simply because the more intimate you are with someone (or Someone) the less you want to offend them – and dare we say, there is more chance of becoming like them.

- Unspoken prayers can be answered.

On one occasion during a powerful time of worship, someone received an urgent prayer request about a developing domestic situation. A Christian couple were having marital problems and the husband was on the verge of walking out – please could we pray? Those leading the worship time felt this would be intrusive and the worship continued uninterrupted. The Lord's presence continued to be strong and no prayers were offered. We heard later that the Lord had miraculously dealt with the situation very soon after the prayer request was received, and those present learned a valuable lesson: sometimes His presence achieves more than our desperate prayers.

- The enemy's plans get frustrated.

The classic example in Scripture is found in 2 Chronicles 20, where Israel was being attacked by a *"great multitude"* [v.2], and the people were really afraid. In response to a prophetic word, Jehoshaphat appointed singers to give thanks to the Lord as they led out the army, to *"sing to the Lord and praise Him in their holy ... garments"* [v.21]. The record states, *"And when they began to sing and to praise, the Lord set ambushments against [those] who had come out against Judah, and they were [self-] slaughtered"* [v.22].

- Light dispels darkness.

Much time and effort has been spent attacking the forces of evil, commanding the darkness to leave, praying out demonic forces and making powerful declarations of truth to challenge the enemy's strongholds. This is all good and well founded on scriptural principles. Yet a simple truth has sometimes been overlooked: that the best way to deal with darkness is not to command it to leave but to switch on the light!

When we worship the Lord, and He begins to inhabit our praises, the light of His presence can present such a challenge to the enemy's darkness that it has to give way. We have seen this to be true – incredibly simple though it sounds.

- Angelic forces are released.

The angels are God's ministering spirits and it seems possible that our worship can release angelic activity on earth and beyond. On several occasions the author has been present when others have seen angels ascending and descending ladders, walking among the worshippers, standing guard over them, and apparently laying hands on their heads.

We could also cite the scriptural example recorded in 2 Chronicles 20:21, where the Lord set ambushments against Israel's enemies, pre-empting a challenging battle. King Jehoshaphat gathered the people together to sing praise to the Lord and the choir marched out before the army chanting, "...give thanks to the LORD, for His mercy and lovingkindness endure for ever." Were these warring angels, released in response to the people's praise?

It may be that our spiritual senses are heightened when we worship, and we 'see' things which exist but are normally unseen – or it may be that our worship hosts angelic presence in a special way. Either way, our awareness of angelic activity is both awesome and encouraging.

What Happens When We Worship?

- Our love increases.

Times of worship can increase our love for the Lord and, in human terms, create a closer 'bonding' in our relationship. At such times we may sense that He is indeed with us and not remote from us, and this can stimulate a deeper love for Him.

- Glimpses of heaven are possible.

It may be because human worship and the worship in heaven are so closely related that times of worship have included glimpses of the heavenly realm – of angels, ladders into heaven, colours, gardens, music, light and other indescribable wonders. Maybe God is giving foretastes of what awaits us, and is excited that we enjoy His presence.

- We shall be blessed.

"He will bless those who ... worshipfully fear the Lord, both small and great" [Ps.115:13].

- God's guidance is promised.

"Who is the man who reverently fears and worships the Lord? Him shall He teach in the way he should choose" [Ps.25:12].

- Close fellowship with God is promised.

"The secret ... [companionship] of the Lord have they who ... (revere and worship) Him, and He will show them His covenant" [Ps.25:14].

†

So many blessings are promised to those who worship God.

But there is a danger here.

Times of worship can have many beneficial side effects for us, but the danger is that our worship can have 'strings attached'. It is possible to engage in times of worship so that we can enjoy the 'side effects'.

We can recognise this in our children when they suddenly become extra helpful, knowing that there is an ulterior motive and we shall soon hear words like, "Please can I have..."

Here are some of the subtle things we can say or think that reveal an ulterior motive in our worship:

In Search of Worship

- "Let's worship to prepare ourselves for hearing the Word."
- "If I worship God, maybe He will heal me."
- At the end of a time of worship someone was heard to say, "I really needed that!" Maybe they did but is that why they came? Did they come seeking a 'boost'?

Matthew records an example of such 'strings attached' worship in Matt.20:20. The mother of Zebedee's children (i.e. her own children!) knelt down before Jesus and worshipped him. There is nothing wrong with that – except that she then asked Him a favour. She wanted her two sons to have priority seats in heaven – one on either side of Jesus!

A selfish request preceded by an expression of worship!

†

Probably all of us have been guilty of worshipping with mixed motives, but we need to guard our hearts so that we worship for His benefit not ours. As a by-product, we shall undoubtedly *be* blessed, but His glory must be our sole motivation.

The roots of this 'cancer' go back into eternity, when Lucifer was not content for God to be the sole beneficiary of worship!

Because God is good, generous and loves to bless, it is not surprising that He will reward us as we worship Him – but worship will always be most pure and acceptable when we come without ulterior motives, however laudable they may be. Let's be sure that we worship Him because He is worth it and not in order to twist His arm for our benefit!

13

What Motivates Our Worship?

You have probably experienced times when there has been an opportunity to worship the Lord with other believers but you felt like doing anything but worshipping. Either you pretend to 'engage' or you make a superhuman effort to feel something spiritual and carry on singing – or perhaps you deflect the attention of others by burying yourself in some Bible passage! This might be a stereotype, but most of us would not claim to 'enter heavenly places' at the drop of a hat (or hymnbook).

So what should motivate us to worship the Lord? What *does* motivate our worship?

†

Worship is an expression of our love for Him, the next question has to be, what *stimulates* our love for Him? Why should we love God?

Is the whole idea of loving an absent, distant, demanding, sin-hating God completely unrealistic? Of course it is! As we previously discussed, you don't love policemen or traffic wardens! And if that is our understanding of the nature of God, worshipping Him will not come naturally.

We also said that from day one, satan's mission has been to discredit God's loving character. He persuaded Eve that God did not have her best interests at heart: "It's better to make your own decisions about right and wrong; God's instructions are not necessary." Satan continues to paint distorted images of God to prevent us from having a loving relationship with Him, convincing us that God is always critical of us because we are sinful. So, the logic goes, we must try harder to please Him and improve the way He sees us. After all, knowing everything about us, how can He love us?

But that is far from the truth, and is perhaps the devil's greatest lie!

In Search of Worship

John says, *"We love Him, because He first loved us"* [1Jn.4:19], and if we fail to understand that God loves us enough to sacrifice His Son for us, we may never find love for Him in our hearts.

So, the first and greatest motivation for us to love God is a realisation of how much He loves us.

His love for us inspires our love for Him. His love for us is not dependent on the degree or consistency of our love for Him. If your heart is bursting with love for Him, His love for you is not increased. Conversely, if you feel anything but love for Him, and your heart is cold, His love for you is not diminished or suspended!

†

If you struggle to believe or accept that God loves you, a few *aide memoire* scriptures might be helpful.

- Remember His past faithfulness to you.

"He is your praise and glory; He is your God, who has done for you these great and awesome things which you have seen with your own eyes" [Deut.10:21].

- Remember the times He has delivered you.

"He reached from on high, He took me; He drew me out of many waters. He rescued me from my strong enemy, and from those who hated me, for they were too strong for me" [Ps.18:16-17].

- Love Him because He has heard your prayers.

"I love the LORD, because He hears [and continues to hear] my voice and my supplications" [Ps.116:1].

- Love Him because He loved you enough to die for you.

"Such hope [in God's promises] never disappoints us, because God's love has been abundantly poured out within our hearts through the Holy Spirit who was given to us. While we were still helpless [powerless to provide for our salvation], at the right time Christ died [as a substitute] for the ungodly. Now it is an extraordinary thing for one to willingly give his life even for an upright man, though perhaps for a good man [one who is noble and selfless and worthy] someone might even dare to die.

But God clearly shows and proves His own love for us, by the fact that while we were still sinners, Christ died for us" [Rom.5:5-8].

- No calamities or suffering can separate you from His love.

"Who shall ever separate us from the love of Christ? Will tribulation, or distress, or persecution, or famine, or nakedness, or danger, or sword?" [Rom.8.35].

- He is not ashamed of you, and counts you as one of His children.

"See what an incredible quality of love the Father has shown to us, that we would [be permitted to] be named and called and counted the children of God! And so we are! For this reason the world does not know us, because it did not know Him" [1Jn.3:1].

- Your love for Him is not what triggers His love for you – your love is a response to the fact that He loves you already.

"Because God bestowed on humanity a free will, man is not forced to love Him, but rather consciously and freely chooses the response he makes to God's love" [1Jn.4:19].

†

So if we are to experience true worship, we need to know that we have a loving God and Father – One Who has our best interests at heart, and Who is honoured to call us his sons and daughters because His Son has already bought us the right to be identified as such.

We continue to be sinful and fail, but God's love does not rise and fall in relation to our success or failure. His goodness is not variable or conditional.

He is loving and He is good – full stop!

In fact, the more conscious we are of our sin and failings, the more likely we are to appreciate His love for us. Jesus explained this to a self-righteous Pharisee who criticised Him for receiving the lavish worship of a local woman, probably a prostitute, saying, *"He who is forgiven little loves little"* [Lk.7:47], and explains that the woman's consciousness of her unworthiness actually prompted her outburst of devotion – devotion to Someone Who accepted her without reproach.

In Search of Worship

It is also worth noting that the Samaritan woman was not so obsessed by her sinfulness that she kept her distance [Jn.4:4-42]. Sometimes we can be so preoccupied with our own unworthiness that we block out God's love and effectively keep Him at a distance. Her focus was on Jesus, not on her own unworthiness.

†

Worship flows out of love. It is not an entity in itself; it is a response.

Sometimes, in our convenient church language, we can view 'the worship' as just another component in our meetings, and lose the sense of being given an opportunity to express our love to God. Sometimes we may have to 'prime the pump' to stimulate the flow of thanksgiving, but if the resulting worship becomes an overflow of grateful hearts it will be accepted and valued by our heavenly Father.

14

Hindrances and Opposition

When we do not feel like engaging in worship, whether individually or corporately, setting aside time for worship can be a real challenge and one in which few of us would claim to be always successful.

So often our minds are preoccupied with other things.

The challenges are endless, and it would be difficult to find someone involved in facilitating corporate worship who has not experienced opposition.

Because our enemy Satan is determined to prevent the Lord from receiving our worship, he has many ways of distracting us, even before we begin to worship.

Below are just a few examples.

- Your preparation time gets crowded out by unexpected domestic crises.
- The car, always reliable, refuses to start as you head off to lead worship.
- The children have minor crises when you are trying to get ready for worship practice.
- An unwanted phone call unsettles you five minutes before you leave home.
- Domestic tensions flare up to cause disunity and delay your departure.
- Worship commitments seem to attract unexpected incidents of sickness and headaches.
- Your computer, normally responsive, malfunctions when you start typing a worship song.

In Search of Worship

- Your printer refuses to take instructions about printing worship music.
- Waves of tiredness come out of nowhere and discourage worship activity!

The author can relate to most of these – and more – and if you are involved in public worship you could probably add to the list.

But beyond the relatively trivial and visible hindrances to our worship, there are more sinister forces at work. Knowing how much our enemy Satan hates true worship, it is hardly surprising that he will do anything to prevent God from receiving the worship He deserves.

A closer look at some of his strategies may be helpful.

†

At the beginning of this book we asked the question, is our enemy Satan actively discouraging our worship? From both the Scriptures and personal experience we know this to be true. Since his ejection from heaven, Satan has sought to frustrate men's worship and divert it to himself. The root of all evil is to be found in his rebellion against God, when he became proud and sought to appropriate to himself the glory and honour due only to God. See Ezek.28 – although not specifically mentioning Satan, this passage seems to describe a glorious heavenly being who fell into the sin of idolatry through pride.

The charge against him is in verse 16: *"Through the abundance of your commerce ... you sinned..."* Satan was 'taking a cut' from the worship to satisfy his own pride, and not directing all of heaven's worship to God.

For this, and this alone, he was cast out of heaven.

And so, his mission ever since has been to prevent man from worshipping God, with plans to set up an alternative kingdom in which only he, Satan, would be worshipped.

†

Another example of 'taking a cut' is recorded in 1Sam.2, where Eli's sons, both priests, were misappropriating the people's sacrificial offerings. In effect, they were taking the choicest parts for themselves – by force if need be – and breaking the Levitical Law. This sin was *"very great before the Lord"*, in that they *"despised the offering of the Lord"* [v.17].

For this sin alone they were killed in battle, even though at the time they were effectively custodians of the ark – which was the visible symbol of God's presence and, they probably presumed or hoped, His protection!

†

The climax of Jesus' temptations in the wilderness concerned the issue of worship. No doubt there were many temptations during those forty days, but Luke records the final three. After suggesting a misuse of Jesus' power to satisfy His own needs, Satan offers Jesus authority over all the kingdoms of the world (and Jesus does not dispute Satan's claim that they are his to give) – on the one condition that Jesus would worship him just once (the aorist tense is used here to denote 'just once').

Jesus replies quoting Scripture, *"It is written, You shall ... worship the Lord your God, and Him only shall you serve"* [Lk.4:8]. (As we saw earlier, 'serve' means to worship or pay homage.)

We can also note in passing that Satan knows, and can quote, Scripture [Ps.91]!

†

In Revelation 12:10 Satan is called *"the accuser of our brethren"* and that he *"keeps bringing before God charges against them day and night"*. So he is making accusations against us to God.

This is reminiscent of Job, the righteous Old Testament character from whom Satan tried to tempt God into withdrawing His favour and blessing. His argument was that if God's favour would be withdrawn, Job would curse God – and this would obviously please Satan immensely! On this occasion the accuser failed.

As the accuser, he often comes to us and tries to convince us that we are not fit to approach God – in prayer or in worship. Accusation leads to condemnation (if we accept his taunts), and if we feel condemned we will probably do what Adam did in the garden of Eden: hide from God's presence behind a tree!

The best way to shake off the enemy's attempts to bring us into condemnation is to remind him of Romans 8:1: *"Therefore, [there is]*

In Search of Worship

now no condemnation ... for those who are in Christ Jesus..." It is very difficult, if not impossible, to approach God in worship if we feel condemned and unworthy.

Thankfully, Satan's days of bringing accusations against us will come to an end and he will be cast out for ever.

†

We should not be surprised therefore that we often encounter opposition when we purpose to worship God. Nothing seems to irritate the enemy more than God's redeemed children making Him the focus of their worship.

We have seen that when Israel was released from Egypt, God's purpose extended far beyond alleviating the pain of His people's slavery. Their release was to facilitate a different kind of serving – a wholehearted commitment to honouring and worshipping God.

Pharoah's strategy for preventing their release is interesting, and we can draw helpful parallels with our own situations, specifically in relation to our commitment to, and preparation for, worship.

We can summarise his tactics and probably identify with some of them in our own lives:

- Keep them busy.

Exodus 5:4 records Pharoah's first response to Moses' demands: "Don't distract the people from their work. In fact, increase their workload, make them get their own materials and beat them when they don't meet their quotas. The work they are doing is important. Stop them thinking about sacrificing to their God by keeping them busy."

We can probably all relate to that one! So many things suddenly seem important when times of worship are approaching.

- Discourage them.

Exodus 5:6-21: "Help them to blame their leaders for their dilemma. If Moses and Aaron had not stirred things up, things would not be so bad. Encourage them to challenge their leaders and they'll get discouraged and stop this 'escape' nonsense!"

Distraction by discouragement – does that sound familiar?

- Give them an easy option.

Exodus 8:25: "If you must sacrifice to your God, do it here in Egypt. Do it in your spare time (which I'll ensure is non-existent!) Fit this worship into your existing schedule."

We must all be guilty of fitting God into our schedules – which the enemy is adept at filling up!

- Let's compromise.

Exodus 8:28: "Go if you must, but don't go far: three days' journey into the wilderness will be tiring and inconvenient. Is this worship really worth the inconvenience of uprooting your families and leaving your homes? Take the easy option: just pop down the road. The alternative will be costly."

We know that true worship will always be costly, and the temptation to minimise the cost will be familiar to many of us – whether of time, money or other commitments.

- Family disunity.

Exodus 10:8: "I'll only let the men go; they're bound to come back if their families remain here, and they can resume work for me. Just think of all the family arguments if I prevent the wives and children from going… They will have to choose between loyalty to their God or to their families."

How many of us have had to face those choices! Satan loves to drive in the wedges as a weapon to destroy unity.

- Minimise the cost.

Exodus 10:24: "Your whole families can go, but your possessions must all remain here under my control. You're bound to return if your wealth and security remain here in Egypt. Surely your god will understand that you can't take everything. You don't need to make this worship thing too expensive."

Another challenge for many of us. What price are we willing to pay in order to worship?

- Maximise any major challenges they face.

In Search of Worship

Exodus 14:5: "I did let them all go in the end, but now I hear they have reached journey's end – the Red Sea! Now's the time to regain control, get them back to work for me and prove this worship nonsense was never a good idea!"

The enemy loves to capitalise on our crises – and to encourage us to blame God just like the Israelites did. Worship was far from their minds at that time, and there is nothing like a good crisis to distract God's people from focussing on worship!

There are of course many other tried and tested tricks to hinder our worship, and there are probably whole demonic departments dedicated to devising new strategies to divert our devotion.

†

Worship has always attracted opposition, and always will, until Satan's power is finally crushed. Until then we can seek to be aware of his tactics and determine to continue offering worship to our Lord – because He is worth it and because He values our love offerings.

15

Unity is Important

Another of the enemy's tried and tested tricks is to cause disunity. He knows that if there are unresolved issues or disagreements between those present, this may well hinder their desire and ability to worship.

"Behold, how good and pleasant it is for brethren to dwell together in unity! It is like the precious ointment poured on the head, that ran down on the beard, even the beard of Aaron ... that came down upon the collar and skirts of his garments ... like the dew of ... Mount Hermon and the dew that comes on the hilla of Zion; for there the Lord has commanded the blessing" [Ps.133].

Where does the Lord *"[command] the blessing"*? Where there is unity. And the converse is also true.

This is a wonderful scripture which has inspired or challenged many of us over the years.

But what is the context?

As part of the Songs of Ascents, it appears just before Psalm 134 – the last of the psalms in the sequence culminating in the arrival of the worshippers at the house of the Lord, where they stand before Him, lift up their hands and bless the Lord.

We can almost imagine the excitement of the pilgrims as they approach the outskirts of Jerusalem and the temple, united in one purpose, all travelling in the same direction, their goal in sight, ready to make their offerings and enter the courts of the Lord. And the Lord enjoys their joy and promises to pour out His blessings.

They bless the Lord, and He blesses them: *"The Lord bless you out of Zion"* [Ps.128:5].

The vertical blessings flow upwards to Him, and blessings descend on the worshippers from the Holy One who inhabits their praise [Ps.22]!

So, unity precedes, and then releases, blessing.

Zion is the place where, according to this Psalm, the Lord releases blessing on His people.

In fact, He *commands* the release of blessing, and this happens in the place where His people are gathered *"in unity"* to worship Him. Is there a secret here?

Many times we ask the Lord for what we desire, or ask for His blessings, and He graciously responds, but it seems that He loves to release His blessings in the context of our worship – in our spiritual 'Zion', where we gather together in unity to worship Him.

We know from Scripture and from personal experience that disunity can be a blockage to worship – and can also prevent the outpouring of blessings from above. According to David in this psalm, unity is both refreshing and sweet-smelling – and wholly acceptable to God.

Other Scriptural Indications that Unity is Significant

The Lord's instructions to Moses concerning the tabernacle were detailed, and included the construction of an ark, a mercy seat and a table for some bread. Twelve buns were to be set on the table in the holy place, and they were to be replaced every sabbath day without fail. They represented the twelve tribes of Israel. The symbolism here is important.

From God's point of view the tribes were always viewed as one – a united people comprised of twelve groups or tribes.

From the priests' point of view, the buns reminded them that they were offering sacrifices on behalf of the whole nation, and not just one specially favoured tribe. The unity of the whole nation was important in the process of offering worship.

†

We have already referred to the dedication of Solomon's temple and the arrival of the ark [2Chr.5]. It was a momentous event of great celebration, and it seems likely that many or most of the four thousand musicians appointed by David were involved. The climax seems to have been an epic musical offering of thanksgiving and praise, which must have been heard beyond the city walls.

It was *"when the trumpeters and singers were ... in unison, making one sound to be heard in praising and thanking the Lord"* [v.13]) that the house of God was filled with a cloud of God's glory and the priests could not stand to carry out their duties.

The implication here is that the unity was not automatic or immediate; it was the result of effort or practice: *"<u>when</u> the..."* Presumably, instruments had to be tuned and musicians had to be allocated their places. Considerable co-ordination must have been required to produce *"one sound ... in praising and thanking the Lord"*. And it was when they produced a united sound – and what a sound that must have been! – that the cloud of God's glory filled the place. The thought of it sends shivers down the spine!

Those times of powerful divine visitation may be rare for us, but they do still happen, and reinforce our understanding that unity is vitally important in worship.

Similarly, the apostles were *"with one accord in one place"* [Acts.2:1, NKJV] when the Holy Spirit was poured out on them.

†

God loves His people to be in unity. Jesus' final prayer to His Father includes a request concerning those who would believe in Him in times to come, that *"they may be one"* [Jn.17:22].

There is undoubtably a special anointing when worshippers gather in unity to worship.

Unity of purpose and unity of relationship – both are important. The enemy loves to divide and cause dissent, and knows better than we do that disunity affects our worship.

May the Lord, through His grace, strengthen us to pursue unity when we purpose to worship Him.

16

Worship Can Be Expensive!

To the question, "Why do you go to church?" the standard answer would probably be, "To worship God." If we were pressed to expand on that statement, we might explain that we go to sing hymns, take communion, listen to edifying teaching, pray, meet friends and, for many of us, contribute to the smooth running of the church's activities. We might also venture to say we go to church to meet with God and enjoy His presence.

But how often do we go to *give*, and not in the hope of receiving blessings, good teaching, good fellowship, answers to prayer, personal ministry and encouragement?

Of course, there is nothing wrong with any of those desires; they are all part of the normal process of our spiritual growth and maturity. And yet, I often wonder how much we actually *give* to God when we gather together.

In some traditions (thankfully less so these days) , the 'giving' consisted of making financial contributions – dropping money into a bag, a box or, at worst, an open plate! (To his shame, the author remembers a time when, whilst visiting a church on holiday, the collection plate was passed round the congregation – in silence, so that others could hear what was being given – and then solemnly presented to the minister to be blessed. Incensed by this tradition, the author's family returned the following Sunday with pockets of full of loose change which were duly deposited in the offering plate. We were never quite sure whether God was amused or disgusted, but we made our point!)

More seriously, if giving to God consists only of making financial contributions, our worship is impoverished.

Worship Can Be Expensive!

Under the old covenant, worshippers always approached God with gifts. No-one was permitted to come empty-handed [Ex.23:15]. Should that challenge us?

The Law made provision for those who were really poor to bring inexpensive gifts – turtledoves or young pigeons [Lev.5:7] – but everyone had to bring an offering. Of course, in context, these were offerings to atone for sin, but thankfully we are no longer under the Law because of the perfect offering Jesus made on our behalf [Eph.5:2; Heb.5:10].

But we are nevertheless encouraged to offer up *"to God a sacrifice of praise"* [Heb.13:15] as our response to His perfect sacrifice, by which we are made acceptable to God.

By definition, bringing an offering is something we consciously *do*, not just a vague belief. As well as our more usual hope of receiving something from Him, we can purpose to bring something to Him in our times of worship. Sometimes that will be easy and sometimes a challenge. In difficult personal circumstances we may find it hard to raise *"a sacrifice of praise"*.

It is good to be aware of the need to *give* to God, as well as to *receive* from Him. In fact, it is almost certain that in giving to Him we shall receive from Him. Our praises rise up to Him and His blessings flow down to us.

He never expects of us more than we can give. And He always accepts what is willingly given.

As we saw, the tabernacle was constructed only of materials which were willingly given by *"those of a generous heart"* [Ex.25:2].

What we offer to Him will primarily be from what He has already given us – our talents, time, resources, finances, giftings and abilities. It is of course possible to employ any or all of those assets for the good of other people or good causes, but if they are offered up to Him as part of our worship they will be accepted.

Valuable gifts are usually expensive. This is no less true in the area of worship. We are encouraged to bring our best to God, not just our fruit and vegetables (remember Cain and Abel)!

Worship can be costly.

In Search of Worship

According to the prophet Malachi, God's complaint about Israel was that the people were making cheap and imperfect offerings in their sacrifices – presumably to minimise the cost [Mal.3:8-10].

†

There are other Scriptural examples of worship being costly.

- We saw the incredible cost Abraham faced when God asked him to offer up his much loved son as a sacrifice.
- When told by the prophet Gad to build an altar in the threshing floor of Ornam [1Chr.21:18], King David insisted on paying the full price for the site, saying he would not offer burnt offerings which cost him nothing [v.24].
- When bringing the ark back to Jerusalem from the house of Obed-edom, David required that regular sacrifices were made throughout the journey – animal sacrifices which he would no doubt have financed. 2Sam.6 records the story.
- Daniel and his three friends paid a high price for refusing to worship idols.
- Elijah endured death threats for crushing idolatry and reinstating true worship.

For many of us, the cost will affect our lifestyle, our relationships, our finances, our time and our priorities. Involvement in worship has been, and continues to be, the most opposed, as well as the most costly, area of ministry. The enemy hates to see the Lord glorified and will spare no effort to prevent Him from being worshipped.

17

Worship and Tithing

This may be surprising to some – and perhaps not welcome news to others – but there is a link between worship and tithing which, as we shall see, is both scriptural and exciting.

For many, tithing has been irksome, an irrelevant condition of a past era and the subject of some sermons which may have made you wish you had stayed at home! For others, it has been a duty, faithfully performed but without joy. And for yet others (possibly fewer in number), it has been a source of blessing and a challenge to try to outgive God.

You may think that tithing had its origins in the Law of Moses and that it has no relevance to us in this present time, but in fact the principle of tithing preceded the precepts of the Law.

The first mention is in Genesis.

Abram returned from a military battle, was met by Melchizedek (a godly priest and also a king) who blessed him, and in response Abram gave Melchizedek a tenth of all the spoils he had taken. No laws were involved and no demands from the priest – just a gesture expressing Abram's appreciation for Melchizedek's provisions and blessing [Gen.14.18].

We are not told why Abram did this, but it does establish an early link between the giving of possessions and provision for the priesthood.

†

There is another interesting link between tithing and the ministry of the priests recorded in Neh.13. You can read the whole story in the earlier chapters, but the priest who had oversight of the temple's storehouses (where the people's tithes and gifts were stored) had a relative who apparently needed accommodation, and the priest allowed him to move in to a room in the temple.

In Search of Worship

This involved clearing out grain, wine and oil etc, which [v.5] were specifically dedicated for the support of the temple staff – and even more importantly, meant removing the frankincense from which the holy incense was made.

Not only was this a violation of an earlier commandment, but the incoming tenant was a man called Tobiah – a man who had vigorously opposed the rebuilding of the city wall and the temple. Allowing this enemy to infiltrate the holy place had consequences for the temple worship. Because the Levites and singers did not receive their normal provisions from the storehouse, they were forced to return to their properties in the country to work for a living, and were therefore not able to serve the Lord and fulfil their duties.

When Nehemiah returned to Jerusalem and discovered what had happened, he evicted Tobiah and all his property, cleansed the storehouse and encouraged the people to fill it again with their tithes of grain, wine and oil, etc. He complained to the officials that the house of God had been neglected, and was quick to ensure that the Levites and singers returned, so that worship could continue.

Surely Jesus must have been mindful of this event when He too cleansed the temple of those who were misusing the place of worship [Matt.21].

†

Worship and tithing come together again in the book of Malachi:

"Bring all the tithes ... into the storehouse, that there may be food in My house, says the Lord, and prove Me now by it... if I will not open the windows of heaven for you and pour you out a blessing, that there shall not be room enough to receive it" [Mal.3:10].

Through His prophet Malachi, God is calling Israel (and specifically the priests) to repent and return to Him. He reminds Israel that they are a chosen nation – but a nation now dishonouring Him by bringing unacceptable offerings to Him in their worship.

They ask God, "How have we dishonoured You?" – and there is a hint of genuine surprise in their question! "Dishonoured You, Lord?" "What – *us*?" [Mal.1:6-7].

The Lord explains that by offering polluted food for sacrifice, they are acting contemptibly.

Offering sick, maimed or blind animals was forbidden by law, but the people (and the priests) were regularly doing so – probably thinking they would keep the best for themselves and, by implication, thinking that God was not worthy of their prime stock.

We already looked at the dangers of 'taking a cut' from worship offerings, and this seems to be another example of people doing just that – getting personal benefit from what should be solely for His benefit.

God challenges the people to try offering shoddy goods in payment of their taxes, and asks what response they could expect from the authorities [Mal.1:8]!

†

So, the issue here is one of bringing unacceptable offerings in worship.

The Lord castigates the priests for leading the people astray, saying that as sons of Levi (the priestly tribe), they had responsibility for the people's worship.

After reminding them of the future return of the Messiah in judgement – when He will purify the priesthood so that they may offer righteous offerings on behalf of the people – He challenges them to return to Him so that He can return to them.

The people respond by asking, *"How shall we return?"* [Mal.3:7].

God's answer is interesting. He tells them that they are robbing Him.

In surprise they ask, "Robbing You, Lord? In what way?"

His answer? "You are withholding your tithes and offerings."

Probably not the answer they expected.

They also learn that they are placing themselves under a curse by doing so. Whilst they were withholding their tithes and offerings, their whole agricultural business operates under a curse, because the ground was cursed when Adam sinned.

†

In Search of Worship

The people were withholding their sacrificial gifts when they came to worship God.

They were weary [1:13]. They complained that they received no benefit from worshipping God, saying, *"It is useless to serve God"* [3:14]. (The word *"serve"* here again means 'to minister to', or 'to worship'.)

God asks the people to bring *"all of your tithes ... into the storehouse"* and then gives them the reason for doing so: *"that there may be food in My house"* [Mal.3:10].

Food for what? Food for whom?

The Levitical Law made provision for the priests to be fed from the people's tithes and offerings. The priests were to offer up the best parts of the people's offerings to God, but they were allowed to eat other parts [Lev.7:35-36]. The priests were sustained by the sacrificial offerings of the people. They had no other income while they were on duty.

So, by not bringing their tithes and offerings to the Lord, the people were depriving the priests of their food – and effectively requiring them to survive on substandard provisions from shoddy offerings or, as we saw earlier, by returning to their fields in the country!

Whilst the central purpose of tithing was to honour God for His faithfulness by gifts of thanksgiving, a practical outcome of not tithing was that the priests would suffer. And the primary task of the priests was to offer sacrificial worship to God on behalf of the people. Tithing enabled the priests to concentrate on their ministry and avoid seeking sustenance elsewhere.

Now we can understand what God meant by bringing food into his house.

(Centuries later, when discussing worship with a Samaritan woman, Jesus says to his disciples, *"I have food ... to eat of which you know nothing"* [Jn.4:32], when they encouraged Him to have lunch. To what was He referring? Is there a sense in which our worship is 'food' to Almighty God? Food for thought indeed!)

†

Thus there was a link between the faithful giving of the people's tithes and the ability of priests to perform their duty as worshippers. This, you may say, is old covenant and no longer relevant. But as the example of Abram shows us, honouring God with a portion of what He has given us does not require us to follow a law – and the practice of doing so can also be beneficial to us because of the promise in Malachi 3:10: *"I will ... open the windows of heaven for you and pour you out a blessing..."*

This promise was given to Israel, but it is one from which we can all still benefit in Christ. There are many documented examples of those who have observed this principle and been abundantly blessed as a result. God is no man's debtor and it is impossible to outgive Him.

Having established that there is a link between tithing and worship, we can now ask whether the tithes we give today are being used to facilitate worship. Do those who administer our tithes understand this principle and prioritise the provision of worship worthy of our great God? Do our tithes sometimes get allocated to prioritise the needs of those around us? Do we understand that originally the tithes ensured that the priests would be provided for, so that they could continue to make offerings on the people's behalf?

There is no other scripture where God invites His people to *"prove"* Him.

There is no other issue in relation to which God promises such lavish bounty on those who test His faithfulness.

If we prioritise worship He will generously provide for our needs.

If we put Him first He has the keys to the windows of heaven and will douse us with heavenly blessings!

18

For His Glory Alone

Most of us would agree that anything which competes with the glory of God is to be avoided.

He says that He will not share His glory with another [Is.42:8]. That is especially true when it comes to our worship.

It is so easy to promote ourselves, our talents and even our names if they are widely known in Christian circles. Whilst there is nothing wrong with using the talents God has given (and of course we should), there is a point where self-promotion can eclipse God-promotion, and nowhere is this more important than in our worship, where everything has to be for His praise and glory.

There have been too many meetings and public events where times of worship have been led by those who apparently enjoy having their talents and personalities on show, and are happy to be the focus of people's attention. Even if they themselves are not conscious of being the centre of attention, it can still be difficult for those present not to focus on what is happening at the front. And how many Christian events are publicised using a well-known name as the one leading the worship – as if to increase attendance or honour the named person? (Of course, most of those 'celebrities' would not seek such promotion, but it happens, and must sometimes encourage a sense of the need to perform.)

If we agree that worship is always addressed to, and focussed on, the Lord, it is worth considering whether anything we do risks drawing people's attention away from Him. There has to be a distinction between a concert and a time of worship. One is a performance of human/musical talent for the entertainment and enjoyment of those who attend (and I have been to many such events and marvelled at the skills of those performing), and the other is (or should be) a corporate offering for the sole benefit of our God because He is worth it.

Some would argue that what we see can inspire worship – a visual as well as an aural stimulus – and the sight of others worshipping, or just being awed by the majesty of a cathedral, can draw out of us an expression of worship; visual inspiration can sometimes be helpful. But we should be aware of the thin line between promoting the glory of God and the performance of men. It is not an easy line to draw, but nevertheless an important one, not least because the issue of diverting glory away from God to anyone or anything else is at the heart of idolatry and the very cause of Satan's expulsion from heaven!

†

I was interested recently to find that in some of the larger churches and cathedrals of our land, the choir is located behind a screen (and sometimes in a balcony) – out of sight of the congregation. Without making too great a point here, in many churches today the worship is led by an individual or team located at the front and in full view of the people.

Are there lessons to be learnt here? Could we envisage times of worship being led by those who are not centre stage and located where they are not the focus of attention?

Those of us who are, or have been, involved in the ministry of worship (or who have responsibility for meetings/events where corporate worship takes place) constantly need to ask ourselves how we can minimise the glory of man and maximise the glory of God!

In the context of a recent Christian gathering, a young worship team impressed me with their undivided focus on the Lord. They were clearly absorbed by the worship they were offering, and there was a total absence of self-promotion. The songs were directed to the Lord and the quality of the music was excellent. Scores of people around them were completely focussed on worshipping the One they loved. It was a holy moment of great purity.

The last song ended, and without hesitation the leader of the meeting stepped forward and in a light-hearted way began to ask the worship leader about the last song, about other songs he had written and about his hairstyle! He was obviously unaware of the awesome moment of worship into which he was intruding. How very sad…

In Search of Worship

For so many, it seems, 'the worship' is just another item on the agenda – a good sing-song to get a meeting off to a good start. Thankfully, it is not always so, but times of worship are seldom valued as the awesome privilege and outpouring of love that they should be.

Time constraints obviously restrict what is possible in many gatherings, but corporate worship seems not to have a high priority in many places.

19

"Me a Priest? Surely Not!"

We have looked at the role of priests in previous chapters, and you may have dismissed the subject as having no relevance to your own life. Perhaps for most of us, the idea of being a priest may not be too exciting (unless of course you happen to be one, looking after a church or diocese) – all that responsibility, the public profile and the ability to do weddings, christenings and funerals; a special calling for a select few, you may think, but not for me!

But whilst this may describe what some of us think of this calling, there is news for those of us who never dream of aspiring to those dizzy heights!

†

The role of the priesthood in the Old Testament is clearly documented, but surely ceased when Jesus made the ultimate sacrifice, replacing the repetitive offerings of the old covenant and giving us direct access to God. The priests had exclusive access to God's presence, but we no longer need them to approach God; the way is now open to all [Heb.10:20-22].

So what relevance could thinking about priests have to our study of worship?

Only this: that we are *all* priests; that is, if our approach to God is based on Jesus' righteousness and not our own.

Does that surprise you?

In one of his letters to believers who were scattered across Asia Minor, the apostle Peter put it this way:

"...you ... are being built up ... a holy priesthood, to offer up spiritual sacrifices acceptable to God through Jesus Christ" [1Pet.2:5, NKJV].

In Search of Worship

Again, in the same chapter, he says, "...you are a chosen race, a royal priesthood ... that you may set forth the wonderful deeds ... of Him Who called you out of darkness into ... light" [v.9].

He is addressing ordinary believers, not clergymen, nor is he writing to Jews as the chosen race, but to anyone who identifies as a family member in God's kingdom.

But what does that mean for ordinary believers like us? In what sense could we be considered a holy priesthood?

†

A brief look at what it meant to be an old covenant priest will be helpful.

- They were priests by 'birth', not personal choice [Ex.40:12-15]. The people could not appoint just anyone to be a priest. All the priests had to trace their lineage back to Aaron; it was an inherited position.

- They were not allocated territory like the other tribes when the Israelites arrived in Canaan, the promised land. Their inheritance was the Lord Himself [Josh.18:7; Deut.18:1-5]. But they were given cities to live in with surrounding pasture land – places to which they would return after completing their tabernacle/temple duties.

- They were exempt from what we used to call 'national service' – not being required to join the army to fight when the Israelites attacked the heathen tribes occupying their land. (In Deuteronomy 20:1-4, the priests are seen preparing the rest of the people for battle, inferring that the priests themselves were not expected to join the army.)

- Their role was to accept what the people brought to God as offerings (there were various kinds), and to prepare them before offering them to God [e.g. Lev.9]. This was often a bloody business as the people brought their livestock to be killed and the animals were cut up into different parts.

- They were the go-betweens [Heb.5:1]. Only the priests were allowed to approach God's presence.

- Only the priests were allowed to carry the ark of the covenant, which was the visible symbol of God's presence with His people [1Chr.15:2].

- After the temple was built, the priests had rooms to stay in, and were fed from the sacrificial offerings of the people whilst on duty.

- Although, perhaps inevitably, there were corrupt priests who abused their office, the nation's spiritual health depended largely on the faithfulness of the priests in making atonement for the people, and ensuring God's favour remained on His people [1Sam.2:12-13].

In short, the Old Testament priests were intermediaries. That was their role, making offerings to God on behalf of the people.

†

All that changed when Jesus, God's sacrificial Lamb, became the once-for-all offering which dealt with the sin problem and made all other sin-offerings unnecessary.

That being so, surely there is no longer a role for the priests?

And yet the New Testament writers pick up the idea of priesthood, calling believers *"a holy priesthood"* and a *"royal priesthood"*.

In what sense, therefore, are we to be priests? Are any sacrifices still necessary? What can we learn here to help us understand our present role as priests?

First, the priests were identified because of their lineage, and so are we. As children of God, we became co-heirs with Christ and have been given new identities with a God-given inheritance. We become priests by inheritance. We do not apply to join the priesthood. We do not get elected. We do not become priests by popular demand. Our spiritual status includes the right to be identified as priests. Furthermore, it is not optional; no-one can opt out in favour of another 'ministry'.

Second, our role as priests takes priority over any 'military service'! Claiming to be preoccupied with fighting the enemy or helping others gain ground in their spiritual walk should not be an excuse for neglecting our priestly 'duties'.

Third, in a sense we have the responsibility of 'carrying the ark' – of ensuring that God's special presence is a priority and that it is treated with due honour. This includes the privilege of engaging in worship, which, as we saw earlier, creates environments which He is pleased to inhabit.

In Search of Worship

Fourth, we are responsible to ensure that sacrifices of praise rise from our lips. This is a huge part of our priestly 'duty', glorifying His name and offering our praise and worship.

†

It is so easy to focus on caring for the needs of others whilst neglecting our privileged responsibility to prioritise worship. Everything the old covenant priests did ensured that God received the offerings and sacrifices of His people.

The writer to the Hebrews tells us, "Through Him, therefore, let us constantly offer up to God a sacrifice of praise, which is the fruit of our lips that ... glorify His name" [Heb.13:15].

And John writes, "To Him Who ever loves us and has ... freed us from our sins by His own blood, And formed us into a kingdom ... [of] priests to His God and Father" [Rev.1.5-6].

He also writes, "...with Your blood You purchased men unto God from every tribe and language and people and nation. And You have made them a kingdom (royal race) and priests to our God" [Rev.5:9-10].

†

So, whether you realised it or not, you are a priest, and tasked with offering up sacrifices of praise to God (assuming you are adopted into His family through faith in Christ).

There is no opt out clause!

What an honour – and what a responsibility! Whatever other responsibilities we may have, or think we have, the responsibility to continue offering up sacrifices of praise and worship should never be neglected.

Enriching the lives of others should never replace honouring the One Who alone is worthy to be praised.

20

What is the Purpose of Church?

The question may surprise you and you may wonder whether this one has any relevance to our exploration of worship, but the short detour will prove to be helpful.

On an individual level, church is a place for fellowship, good teaching, community and identity. It also may be a place to invite friends who are interested to find God.

On a corporate level, church is a resource for reaching out to our communities with the gospel, a place of prayer and a base for mission initiatives to other countries, to mention just a few of the aspects which identify many local churches.

Few of us would argue that a healthy church would not be providing many of the above.

Church will mean different things to different people – and also what it means to us can change in different seasons. For example during the lockdowns that marked the outbreak of the Covid virus, many churches had to rethink their activities and cancel meetings.

But from a broader perspective, what is the *purpose* of church? For what does it exist?

†

Why do we meet together as members of God's family?

Does church exist for our benefit?

Does it exist to evangelise the world?

Does it exist for God's benefit?

In Search of Worship

It is worth looking at the scriptural evidence to see what God had in mind when He spoke about 'church', and to examine the foundation on which all church activity should be built.

†

There is no mention of church in the Old Testament. The first mention is in Matthew's Gospel where Jesus says He will build His church [Matt.16:18].

Whilst some have claimed that Jesus meant us to understand that Peter himself would be the rock on which He would build the church, I believe He was speaking about Peter's confession that Jesus was the Christ, Son of the living God. The Amplified Bible (AMPC) expands on the passage as follows:

"And I tell you, you are Peter [Greek, Petros – a large piece of rock], and on this rock [Greek, petra – a huge rock like Gibraltar] I will build My church…"

It is to the latter that Jesus refers when He speaks of the foundation of His church – the confession that He is the Christ. On *that* foundation everything about church depends .

So from the beginning we can understand two things about church:

- Jesus says that church is something which will be built – a structure which will be formed over time, not just created instantly.
- Jesus says that church is something which *He Himself* will build. Thankfully, He did not say it would be up to us to build it!

There is clearly a divine plan as to its design, construction and purpose.

†

Perhaps the most common perception about the identity and function of church concerns its role as the *"body of Christ"*. Several scriptures support this truth:

- *"Now you are the body of Christ"* [1Cor.12:27, NKJV].
- *"Christ is the "supreme Head of the church … Which is His body"* [Eph.1:23].
- *"He also is the Head of [His] body, the church"* [Col.1:18].

What is the Purpose of Church?

Clearly, the church is not autonomous and self-governing; it remains dependent on the Head and exists to fulfil the purposes of Christ, the Head.

Writing to the Corinthian believers, Paul explains that God has appointed various ministries within His church, each with its own identity and role, much like the parts of a human body, and says that as the parts work together, church will grow and function smoothly [Eph.4:16]. It is easy to conclude from these scriptures that the church, Christ's body on earth, exists only to be productive – to work hard until He returns, establishing His kingdom in His absence. But we shall see that this is not the case.

So we can see, based on several scriptures, that the church exists to carry out the wishes of Christ, the Head.

However, few of us would claim that everything the church does qualifies as a response to clear instructions from the Head! We tend to muddle on, doing the best we can, doing what we think the Head would want us to do. Some of His instructions are clear and broadly timeless, but others may be less clear, or specific to particular situations.

Many of us would thus define the church's role as a body implementing the wishes of the Head – whilst not claiming to get it right all the time.

†

The word in the Greek translated *"church"* means 'called out ones' (*ekklesia*), and implies that the people who comprise church would in some sense be those who had a separate identity from those around them. If this meant that church members would instantly be plucked out of normal life, called away to higher things, you and I would obviously have missed the boat because we are still here! Some streams have taken this to mean that a monastic life is implied, or that we should be a separate and distinct society, like, for example, the Amish.

God's plan was that His church would be comprised of individuals who would in some sense have a separate identity from those around them, and corporately would form a spiritual body with Christ as its Head.

The common understanding of church as 'that building on the corner with a steeple' is therefore considerably wide of the mark. Jesus' church would be built of *people* – people who understood Who He was and made that belief their confession.

†

Jesus spoke only briefly about His church whilst on earth. Before His death and resurrection it would not have made much sense to His followers, and its formation would only take place after Jesus completed the work of salvation on the cross.

But it is clear from the book of Acts, and other scriptures, that the early church consisted of groups of people drawn together by their common belief that Jesus was the Messiah and the Son of God. In those early days, the church grew quickly. In Acts 2:47 we read that *"the Lord added to the church daily"* [NKJV].

However it was not a popular group to belong to. The religious establishment, led by Saul the zealous Pharisee, was determined to wipe it out at any cost, because the idea that Jesus was the Messiah did not fit with their rigid understanding of the Law. You did not declare your identity as a church member unless you were willing to suffer torture or death for your belief.

This was the early church. The apostles proclaimed Who Jesus was, and people chose to stake their lives on this 'rock', often at great personal cost.

As the word about Jesus spread, local groups were formed and leaders were appointed. Some were commissioned to proclaim the good news in other places and other countries.

Others had specific ministries within the local churches. From his writings, we know that Paul was commissioned, not only to evangelise and plant churches, but also to explain to believers the implications of their new-found faith, and to give spiritual guidance to the young churches. His pastoral letters form much of our New Testament and reveal much about God's plan for His church.

From these letters, we get the feeling that the Holy Spirit could hardly wait to reveal to Paul what God had in mind for His church. Paul's Holy-Spirit-inspired insights into the purpose of church are both exciting and challenging.

What is the Purpose of Church?

†

We have seen that scripturally the church exists to be the body of Christ on earth. Until everything is brought into submission under Christ's rule, there is much to be done on earth: combatting evil, establishing His kingdom, releasing people from the bondage of sin and working for the maturity of God's people, to mention just a few challenges. We could liken the role of church to that of the servants in Jesus' parable – holding the fort until the Master returns, trying to be productive and faithful, and looking for that final accolade of, *"Well done, thou good and faithful servant"* [Matt.25:21, KJV].

But there are other aspects of church which often get overlooked.

If we are right in understanding the only role of church as working on God's behalf until Christ returns, there would be no purpose for its existence after Christ's second coming. It would have achieved its purpose and could be disbanded. Church would be shipped off to heaven and no longer have a meaningful identity!

But according to the Scriptures there is no dissolution date for church once Christ's reign is established. As suggested earlier, church has an ongoing purpose beyond its servant role on earth – which might come as a surprise.

In Ephesians Paul writes, "[The purpose is] that through the church the ... many-sided wisdom of God ... might now be made known to the angelic rulers ... in the heavenly sphere" [Eph.3:10], and, "To Him be glory in the church ... throughout all generations and forever and ever" [Eph.3:21].

Corporately, as well as individually, we are a testimony to God's wisdom and grace. Church provides an ongoing demonstration to principalities and powers of God's plan, that salvation is by His grace alone and is not dependent on human achievement. Church will be the evidence of God's generosity in redeeming mankind – evidence, both now and through eternity, that God is not only good and righteous but merciful and gracious. This is an eternal calling, broader than 'working in the vineyard' until the master returns.

†

In Search of Worship

There is another dimension to the role of church which is easy to overlook.

Revelation speaks about the marriage of Christ, the Lamb, to the bride, about whom the Bible speaks as having *"prepared herself"* [Rev.19:7].

The bride will be dressed in dazzling white linen (speaking of righteousness) and be comprised of God's people – surely speaking of the church.

The church is never called the *wife* of Christ. Wives, without implying any sexist stereotype, are partners who contribute in many practical ways to the success of an ongoing relationship, and husbands obviously value their wives' abilities as well as their physical appearance. But on their wedding day, the bridegroom has little interest in his bride's cooking skills or management experience; he is, quite rightly, absorbed by her beauty and by his love for her. It is an amazing thought that the Lord will be consumed by the beauty of His bride – the incredibly transformed body of His church, clothed in His righteousness and without spot or blemish. Hopefully you will be there!

So the time will come when 'church' becomes 'bride' and is presented to the Bridegroom. At this present time God is preparing His Son's bride, ready for that great occasion.

It is all too easy to be so preoccupied with our duties as servants that we miss the eternal calling of being His bride. It is an exciting prospect, and one which could inspire us if we ever wonder what church is all about – speaking of Christ's universal church and not the building on the corner!

†

A further aspect of the identity and function of church brings us back to our present challenge to understand worship.

Paul, writing to the believers at Ephesus, explains that they are being built up into a spiritual structure, to be a sanctuary dedicated to the presence of the Lord.

"In Him the whole structure is joined ... together ... and it continues to rise (grow, increase) into a holy temple in the Lord ... [to be a] (dwelling place) of God ... (by ...) the Spirit" [Eph.2:21-22].

This is the church – gradually rising up from the foundation of the apostles and prophets – a building still in formation but which will finally be completed when all the building blocks are in place. Peter echoes the same thought: *"[Come] and, like living stones, be yourselves built [into] a spiritual house"* [1Pet.2:5].

This is not speaking about the future. This is still happening, now and to us, if we have accepted Christ's gift of righteousness for salvation – and is as much a privilege as it is astounding. We are building blocks in a spiritual temple – all our different shapes and identities somehow being fitted together to form a dwelling place for Almighty God, by the Spirit.

†

But what normally happens in a temple? For what purpose does a temple exist?

Biblically, temples were places where the priests carried out their work of offering the people's sacrifices to God – facilitating the people's worship.

The idea of a temple being a place of worship is common to several of the world's religions. Temples were built to be places of worship. Any other function they may have had was secondary to their primary purpose of facilitating corporate worship. Of course, we no longer have to visit geographical locations to worship God, because of Jesus' perfect offering on our behalf, but we also know that Scripture encourages us to continue to offer sacrifices of praise and thanksgiving!

So, the Lord is in the process of forming a spiritual temple – a place from which worship will ascend from His people. On one of His visits to the temple, Jesus evicted those who had made it a place of commerce, and were making personal gain from those who came to worship. This, more than anything else, ignited His righteous anger – that the temple had ceased to be a place solely dedicated to the worship of His Father.

Churches, therefore, are local groups of believers who are gradually being built into a vast spiritual temple – a place from which worship rises to God, and a place which God delights to inhabit.

†

In Search of Worship

We miss out if our understanding of church is solely as a work force seeking to evangelise the world. Some think of the church as God's employment agency, working to establish His kingdom on earth. Whilst there is some truth in this point of view, it does not tell the whole story. If 'working in the vineyard' is our sole *raison d'être*, we will tend to focus all our energies on being effective servants.

Sadly, a look around many churches would suggest that nothing else features on their agendas. But if we understand that our high calling includes preparing ourselves for being Christ's bride, if we understand that our calling is to be building blocks in a structure built for His habitation, and if we understand that we exist to be a worshipping body, we may need to re-evaluate our priorities and adjust our mindsets.

†

Does all this begin to answer our original question, what is the purpose of church?

Whilst we may not consciously contribute much to the bridal preparations [Rev.19:7] or think of ourselves as prize exhibits demonstrating God's amazing grace [Eph.3:10], we can add our voices to the universal offerings of praise and worship which continue to rise from His spiritual temple – which is His church.

There is far more to being church than being His labourers on earth!

21

Which Jesus Will You Worship?

This question is not as ridiculous as it might at first sound. In fact, it might just be the most important question in this book.

Even in our post-Christian culture, most people know who Jesus was, although the answers will vary as to His relevance to their lives. But even within Christian circles, there is some ambiguity about His identity and its implications for our lives and worship.

†

In many churches these days there is a strong emphasis on social action, where the focus is on reaching out into the local community to share God's love in practical ways. There is nothing wrong with that of course, as Jesus taught that His disciples would be *"salt"* and *"light"* in their communities [Matt.5:13-14], and the apostle James wrote about the need for faith to be expressed in practical ways.

We have food banks, accommodation for the homeless, support groups for the lonely, clubs for local children, youth groups and coffee mornings, to name just a few, and it seems that there is a fresh awareness of the church's commitment to impact local communities. This, surely, is what churches should be about – sharing the good news of God's love with those who need to hear, in a variety of practical ways. Jesus' teachings provide a clear basis for the way we live, and His earthly ministry is an example to us all.

For many people Jesus is, above all, our example – someone to follow, the perfect role model for us, both individually and corporately, as we live our lives and seek to care for those around us. But sadly, this is the extent of many people's understanding of Jesus – Who He was and what He did.

In Search of Worship

He was a good man for sure, and an excellent teacher and moral guide. Even during His earthly ministry, there were those who gladly acknowledged Him as such – as a wise teacher or rabbi – but failed to recognise Him as their Lord, the One Who came to be their Saviour.

There are many today who can accept Jesus as a perfect role model and good teacher, even if they find His teachings to be extremely challenging!

If He is seen as only, or primarily, a teacher and example, it is easy to see how He could fit into the framework of interfaith discussions, alongside other wise men whose teachings have been influential. If the purpose of His coming was to improve our lives by good advice, and not to achieve salvation and deal with the issue of man's sin, He would be relatively harmless to those who think differently, and in no way a threat!

His identity as Saviour and Lord is far more demanding than His identity as a good teacher and perfect example.

So we can ask, which is the Jesus Who should be the subject of our worship?

Is it Jesus the teacher, the moral inspiration, the perfect example of manhood which everyone should seek to emulate – or the Jesus Who laid down His life at great cost to secure our eternal salvation?

I believe there currently is a real danger of embracing the former Jesus and neglecting the real message of His coming. Focussing on the teachings and social implications of His teaching can easily overshadow the deeper message of salvation which those around us need to hear. The awakened social conscience of many churches (and individuals) can so easily eclipse His identity as our Saviour and Lord. Ministering to the needs of those around us can so easily deflect us from worshipping the very One Who is the source of forgiveness and new life.

†

The Scriptures are clear about the reason His Father sent Him to earth.

God did not send His Son to be a great teacher. He did not send His Son just to improve the lives of those who were struggling. He did not send Him as an example to be followed, nor did He send Him to rule an earthly kingdom (although He will come again to establish righteousness on earth).

He sent Him to be a Saviour.

Gabriel, no less, revealed to Mary that she would have a son: "She will bear a Son, and you shall call His name Jesus, for He will save His people from their sins" [Matt.1:21].

The message the angels brought to the shepherds was, *"...to you is born this day ... a Savior, Who is Christ ... the Lord"* [Lk.2:11].

When His parents presented Him at the temple, according to the Levitical Law, a godly man called Simeon prophesied over Jesus and said, *"...with my [own] eyes I have seen Your Salvation"* [Lk.2:30]. Here *"salvation"* means 'the one who saves'.

John the Baptist introduced Jesus to the crowds around him as *"the Lamb of God"* [Jn.1:29] referring to Jesus' sacrificial death to deal with the issue of man's sin once and for all.

In all these prophetic revelations, Jesus is identified as the One Who would deal with the sin issue, the Saviour, and not as a prophet, teacher or example.

In their doctrinal letters to young churches, the apostles hardly mention Jesus' teachings or the perfection of his earthly life. Their message is primarily about the glorious benefits resulting from His redemptive work on the cross. Jesus' legacy for them was all about purchasing our salvation and its eternal significance. To have held Him up as an example to be followed, or a teacher to be studied, would have completely missed the point, and have denigrated the One Who gave His life to buy man's salvation as such incredible cost.

If Jesus' example and teachings represented the substance of His appearance, surely the New Testament could have ended after the four Gospels! What would be the point of subsequent books, except to expand on and apply what He taught?

†

When John was permitted to peep into the realm of heaven, he saw and heard what the angels and heavenly beings were saying and singing. They were worshipping the Lamb and speaking of His sacrificial offering to redeem mankind – because of which He was entirely worthy to be worshipped.

In Search of Worship

Nothing has changed in heaven; the angels are still worshipping Him as the Lamb of God Who is always worthy of worship. They do not praise Him for His wisdom or His humility in going to earth. Their focus is always on His worthiness as Saviour and the Creator of all things.

It is *this* aspect of His life which gives inspiration to *our* worship. We worship the One Who did for us what we could not do for ourselves – not the One Who showed us what we should strive to become!

†

Two parallel Jesuses.

One sent as the teacher, the example, the moral inspiration, the perfect life to be emulated, showing us how to live, how to love and care for others etc.

The other, the Lamb of God, the Saviour, the source of our righteousness and new life.

If we see only the former, our lives will be preoccupied with doing the best we can and serving others. It is not impossible to worship Jesus as a great teacher and example, but such worship would arise from respect rather than love.

It is because He came to save us, paying such a high price for us, that we understand God's love for us and respond out of our love for Him. True worship is always inspired by love, not duty or respect.

If we understand that He has made possible our escape from Satan's grip, into the liberty of being acceptable members of God's family, by laying down His perfect life on our behalf, our natural response will be to worship Him. And when that is our priority, as God's love is poured into our hearts, it will inevitably flow out to those around us [Rom.5:5].

Seeing Who Jesus is – our Lord and Saviour – will inspire our worship. Even the angels recognise that His worthiness is due to His work of salvation, and make this the theme of their song:

"You are worthy ... for You were slain ... and with Your blood purchased men unto God from every tribe and language ... and nation. ... Deserving is the Lamb, Who was sacrificed, to receive all the power ... and honor and ... (glory)" [Rev.5:9,12].

22

Progression in Worship

The idea of a progression in worship may seem surprising to some, particularly to those who are used to the format where hymns are interspersed with readings, prayers and the sermon.

Of course, there is more of a sense of progression in liturgical services, where the format leads those present along a well-trodden path – leading in many cases up to the preaching of the Word. In other streams, individual hymns may sometimes be related to the theme of the sermon, but in my experience they have seldom contributed to a flow of subject matter in the corporate worship. We may not all agree that this is important.

Even when the songs or hymns are grouped together (as they often are in modern meetings), the selection of songs rarely exhibits a sense of progression in their content, although this has been more widely understood in recent years.

So, is it helpful to think about progression in our corporate worship?

†

In Psalm 95 (and the pastoral references suggest that David was probably the author), there are hints at a useful progression in worship:

- *"...come before his presence with thanksgiving"* [v.2];
- *"...make a joyful noise ... with songs of praise!"* [v.2];
- *"...worship and bow down and kneel before the Lord"* [v.6].

Psalm 100 has a similar thought:

- *"Enter into His gates with thanksgiving"* [v.4];
- *"Enter ... His courts with praise"* [v.4].

In Search of Worship

The reference here is to the tabernacle, which was divided into three parts: the entrance courtyard, the holy place and the holy of holies.

Thankfully, if we have put our trust in Jesus for our salvation, we no longer have to observe the rituals of tabernacle worship, as we have all been made priests and can enter the presence of God on the basis of Jesus' perfect sin offering – and God invites us to do so boldly and frequently!

But the three-part model suggested in the Psalms can still be helpful to us.

- Thanksgiving is the proper response to an appreciation of God's love, mercy, forgiveness and generosity, and is a good theme with which to enter His *"gates"*.

- That in turn leads us to a broader understanding of His character, majesty and power, which naturally turns into praise as we enter His *"courts"*.

- We give praise for Who He is and what He has done, which inevitably leads into a more intimate response of worship when we enter His intimate presence and, to quote the Psalm, *"worship and bow down, and kneel before the Lord our Maker"*.

In recent times, some worship leaders have found this a useful progression – a journey which leads worshippers into the awesome presence of God.

This is not to imply that praise and worship will only occur when this pattern is followed. Spontaneous thanksgiving may not lead to anything else but be totally acceptable!

Praise may erupt from our hearts at any time. And worship needs no context except a heart of love!

But the pattern has proved to be useful, especially in times of public worship.

†

The idea of 'progression' in our worship is not new.

Some Psalms (120-134) are known as Songs of Ascents and trace the journey of pilgrims up to Jerusalem for the feasts.

(In passing, we can note that before leaving home they complain about their challenging ungodly environment, whereas when they enter God's house their focus changes and they are consumed by the joy of worshipping Him. Sometimes worship can change our perspective and lift us above our immediate problems.)

†

We know that the Old Testament records many things which were typical and which find fulfilment in the new covenant.

In the detailed description of Moses' tabernacle in the wilderness, the process of approaching God was clearly defined, and while we are no longer bound by those regulations, we can learn from the principles behind the regulations, and understand more clearly what was accomplished by Jesus on our behalf when He became the perfect sacrifice.

We already noted the three divisions of the tabernacle – the courtyard, the holy place and the holy of holies – and have also mentioned the three stages of worship which we find in the Psalms – thanksgiving, praise and then worship – but the design of the tabernacle and the details of its furnishings can also teach us much about worship.

This is a huge subject and worthy of detailed study, but a summary is helpful:

- According to Numbers 2, the tribe of Judah (the name means 'praise') camped to the east of the tabernacle, toward the sunrise, and was the first tribe to set out when the people broke camp.
- Then the people encountered the burnt altar, which signifies the cross and prompts our thanksgiving for what Jesus accomplished for us.
- The next object was the bowl of water, signifying the washing of the Word. We worship in truth as well as in spirit, acknowledging the truth of His word.
- The journey continued into the holy place – a place with no natural light, only the candlestick, representing the Spirit. Revelation increases as we get closer to the holy of holies, still worshipping in spirit and truth.

In Search of Worship

- The twelve buns on the table [Lev.24:5] speak of the unity of the twelve tribes, as we saw in chapter 15. For us today, it reminds us that we are united in Christ, one church, and there is no place for flouting 'tribal' preferences or identities.

- Finally, in the place reserved for the priesthood (now us!) there is intimacy with God and everything is vertical. This is not the place to focus on human needs.

The goal of our worship journey is His presence, in which human needs and preoccupations melt away.

Just as in the realm of human love, where there can be stages of intimacy preceding complete fulfilment, there can be a process of entering God's presence which honours Him and which allows us to express our love for Him more deeply. It is true that we are invited to come boldly and to enter in without hesitation, but it is possible to overlook the awesome privilege we have of drawing near by rushing in 'with our boots on', so to speak!

Again, to draw parallels from our human experiences, it is honouring to those we love if we do not take free access for granted!

So it is helpful to consider our worship as a journey into God's holy presence, even if at times we do just barge in like impetuous children demanding His immediate attention. And even when we do, by His amazing grace we still receive a warm welcome!

23

The Use and Misuse of Music

Music is not worship, and worship is not music!

To expand on that blindingly obvious statement, there can be worship without music, just as there is music which is manifestly not worship!

But there has always been a strong link between the two, and it is worth exploring their relationship in the context of our present search for true worship.

†

Music has always been important – in both primitive societies and developed civilisations.

It has played a dominant role in all the great cultures of the world – in ancient China, in Greek mythology, in Jewish history and in the folklore of many primitive tribes around the world.

In the secular world, the use of music has dramatically changed in recent times. To highlight just two examples: most TV commercials involve the use of background music; and most shops have music playing to encourage us to relax and purchase their goods.

The civilised world has not only made music more widely available, it has made it difficult to avoid. All kinds of music are now available to anyone who has an electronic device, walks into a shop or switches on their radio (and that is virtually everyone).

But for centuries this was not the case.

†

Through the years music has been used for many things. Below are just a few.

- It has played an active part in the hunting rites of some tribes.

In Search of Worship

- It was employed to celebrate the passing agricultural seasons.
- It has been used to summon warriors preparing for battle.
- Its magical powers have been evoked to produce healing.
- It has been widely used to invoke the presence of spiritual powers in witchcraft.
- It has been a stimulus for those striving to enter a state of trance in some religious ceremonies.
- It is known to boost sales on the high street.
- Therapists have used it to help us relax.
- It entertains us.
- In many cultures the basic human experiences of birth, marriage, bereavement and death are accompanied by appropriate music – and in parts of Africa, the moment a person leaves this world for another is marked by a tinkling bell!
- In Indian culture, the earliest references to music have a religious context – involving hymns to various gods.
- It is widely used to make money, with many artists enjoying substantial rewards from the sale of their music.
- It has also been the route by which a musician can quickly become famous.

†

It would seem that in some form or other, music has been used to express every aspect of human life, and the fact that it features so prominently in divine worship should not surprise us.

In the biblical record, the first mentioned musician was Jubal. It says, *"...he was the father of all those who play the lyre and pipe"* [Gen.4.21]. Jubal predated the great flood, so his family's talents obviously passed down through Noah's family.

But music did not start with Jubal!

In the heavenly realm music was important before man was created.

Ezekiel 28 records God's pronouncement of judgement on the king of Tyre, and many biblical commentators have seen this as referring to Satan himself, expressing himself in, or typified by, a proud earthly king.

If that interpretation is correct, Satan is described as having within himself the ability to make music (his *"timbrels and pipes"* [Ezek.28:13, NKJV]), and it is possible that he had responsibility for heaven's worship. Instead of ensuring that the music focussed on God, he became obsessed with his own beauty, and diverted it to glorify himself.

His sin is recorded as passing on goods for personal profit. Could that describe what was happening in the area of music and worship – he was diverting worship to exalt himself? Was he saying that God was not worthy of receiving all of heaven's worship?

There is a serious warning here for all of us who are involved in corporate worship: anything which diverts worship away from God and exalts our own talents or personality is unacceptable – and dangerous!

We can wonder whether Satan's removal had a serious effect on heaven's worship, but thankfully, when St John gets a glimpse into heaven [Rev.4:8-11], he sees that true worship is continuing. Songs are sung and music is played, and God is at the centre of it all.

†

So music is not confined to earth and to those of us who live on it. In fact, according to Job 28, the stars sing!

God asked Job some questions when he questioned God's wisdom, and one of His questions was, "Where were you when the morning stars sang together and all the sons of God shouted for joy?"

And if the stars sing, what about the nightingales and the blackbirds and the whales?

Would it be fanciful to imagine that God built music into the very fabric of creation, and we have yet to tune in to its rich variety? Science is beginning to reveal some of these mysteries, and hopefully, all will be revealed when we cease to *"know in part"* [1Cor.13:12].

†

In Search of Worship

Returning to the biblical sequence of recorded music, we find Moses and the Israelites singing a song *"to the Lord"* {Ex.15:1} after their deliverance from Egypt.

Then in Numbers 21:17, the people sang a song called *"Spring up, O well"* as they travelled through the desert.

Next, in Deuteronomy 31:19, God tells Moses to write down a song and teach it to the people. It was a song which would remind them of God's covenant with them, and challenge them when they fell into idolatry. Moses wrote it down the same day and taught the people!

It is not perhaps a worship song, but a song with a clear purpose and a song originating from God Himself!.

Judges 5:1 records Deborah, the people's judge, and Barak singing a song about God's victories.

David [2Sam.22] celebrated God's intervention and victory in a song which is recorded in full – and parts of which are still sung today.

When King David was instructing his son Solomon regarding the temple he would build, David specified which instruments should be used and gave the names of the leading musicians who were all known to be skilful in offering praise to the Lord. (Not many musicians could claim notoriety after three thousand years, but the names of these worshippers has been preserved for us. Does this hint at God's priorities?)

There are other scriptural examples of music being used in various ways: to celebrate events, instruct the people, call warriors to battle, worship God, summon the people, sooth troubled spirits and to express the many human emotions we find in the book of Psalms.

There is even a reference in the Old Testament to God Himself singing. The prophet Zephaniah writes, *"The Lord your God ... will rejoice over you with joy. ... He will exult over you with singing."* [Zeph.3:17} Have you ever thought of Almighty God as bursting into song? And, even more amazingly, singing about his people! Obviously, this is a prophetic reference, but an encouraging one because you don't normally sing about things that disappoint you or about which you are embarrassed!

†

The Use and Misuse of Music

It is interesting to consider the relatively slow development of music (especially religious music) in our Western culture over the last two thousand years and to compare that with the highly developed musicality of King David and his thousands of temple musicians many centuries earlier. The contrast is immediately obvious.

We can presume that as Israel strayed into idolatry and true worship declined, so too the prominence of skilled music based at the temple also declined. The destruction of the first temple and exile of the Jews into Babylon during the sixth century BC must have had a negative effect on the continuation and development of religious music – and their sadness and frustration is evident in one of the Psalms of the time:

"By the rivers of Babylon, there we ... sat down, yes, we wept ... On the willow trees ... we hung our harps ... they who led us captive required of us a song ... saying, Sing us one of the songs of Zion. How shall we sing the Lord's song in a strange land?" [Ps.137:1-4].

The destruction of the second temple in AD 70 also had its effect, fragmenting the worship into local synagogues, where there would have been limited resources to produce quality music.

Whatever the reasons, we can say that King David's temple worship represented a high point in the history of religious music which has probably yet to be equalled.

†

It is beyond the scope of this book to look in detail at the development of church music through the ages, but there are early examples of canticles (sung passages of Scripture like the 'Magnificat') and hymns (which St Augustine defined as "the praise of God by singing") and the Psalms.

Much has been written about the dual, but largely separate, development of folk music and of church music. The two streams seem to have existed alongside each other with very little overlap for centuries, due in part to the absence of any system of musical notation until at least the ninth century.

Folk music was usually unstructured and passed down orally.

In Search of Worship

Church music had its roots in the Jewish culture and the early plainsong format of what is now the Roman Catholic mass. The '*Te Deum*', still used in Roman Catholic liturgy, was originally a Latin hymn of praise addressed *to* God (not a hymn *about* Him), and meaning, literally, "Thee, God, we praise." According to some historians, the first function of music in the early Middle Ages was the praise of God and His saints.

How things have changed!

In the Middle Ages music gradually developed outside the confines of the church, and in particular into the realms of the royal courts and nobility. Increasingly linked to formal dance and entertainment, the music of that time embraced new forms, new instruments and a wider public. But it was a slow and gradual process.

As we saw in an earlier chapter, church music became a means of communicating truth and doctrine, especially to congregations with little or no reading ability.

Still later, it was a useful medium for expressing personal religious experiences.

†

And so we come to the present day, when music permeates the lives of most people and society in general. But in many ways its function has changed.

In secular society, music which could once be enjoyed only at specific places and at particular times is now available to anyone and at any time. Whether that is a good thing or not is debatable.

Certainly, it is now common for music to provide a background sound while we do other things, and for some people this is not only normal but essential! Some people cannot work unless they have background music. Others find it intrusive and annoying.

One side effect of this constant dependence on background music is that silence is uncomfortable. Another is that constant musical noise can affect our ability to think clearly. Yet another is the restriction it imposes on live human interactivity; many people walk around with earphones providing constant musical sound and seem to be beyond the reach of normal conversation!

The Use and Misuse of Music

Does all this devalue music? Are we becoming desensitised to *real* music?

†

What relevance does all of this have to our search for true worship? What has its effect been on Christian / church music and, more specifically, on our present-day worship?

There are endless CDs and DVDs featuring Christian music and musicians, and for many people they provide enjoyment, encouragement, inspiration and instruction.

It is undoubtedly better to be listening to such edifying music than the unending output of secular music which invades our daily lives.

Using worship songs as background music whilst doing other things can sometimes stimulate our own worship and also be uplifting, but if the song happens to be, for example, a love song to the Lord, and we are engaged in another activity whilst mindlessly joining in, could that be dishonouring to Him?

At the time of writing, a well-known secular music group has been in the news for banning mobile phones at their concerts. The reason given? The musicians were finding it hard to know whether the audience was paying attention and engaging with their music or were primarily focussed on taking selfies and brandishing their recording devices!

In our times of worship, does the Lord sometimes notice our distractions and wish our focus could be solely on Him? If we are honest, the times when He gets our undivided attention are probably quite rare, but there is something disturbing about the fact that we can mix our genuine offerings of love with unrelated activities, just because Christian CDs make good background music.

To draw a parallel in our human experience, many intimate moments during love-making have been ruined by verbalising a thought about tomorrow's meeting at the office or a late addition to the shopping list. There are special times when trivial intrusions are out of place, and the same can be true in our times of worship – whether corporate or private.

†

In Search of Worship

Another effect of the music-all-the-time culture is that we are increasingly dependent on entertainment. It is possible to live with a non-stop diet of music, and many people do.

What effect can this have on our Christian meetings?

Some churches excel at providing quality music and spare no expense when it comes to visual presentation. Certainly, God is worthy of our best at all times. And yet, in corporate worship there can sometimes be a point at which the focus shifts from God to entertainment. It is possible to have a 'worship time' in which everything is technically, visually and musically excellent, but where the Lord has not been the centre of our attention. I sometimes wonder whether the musicians tasked with offering temple worship in David's time faced the same challenges!

The responsibility for centring our attention on the Lord must surely be shared between us as individuals and those 'at the front'. The Lord knows our hearts – and the hearts of those who lead. This is not to encourage us to be critical, but if we are sensitive to the Spirit, we will know in our hearts when that line has been crossed.

†

Much of the above has dealt with the misuse of music, but we also need to look at some aspects of its rightful use – especially in the context of worship.

Music has the capacity to express a wide range of emotions. This is evident from the work of great composers like J.S. Bach (his 'Passions'), Handel ('Messiah') and many others. Heights of exuberant praise mix with depths of pathos and anguish. Music can move us to tears or get us dancing! And there is no reason why these reactions should not be expressed in our worship. We saw that the Psalms encourage us to sing, shout, dance, clap and kneel before God, and we would have to concede that we British are not always good at such physical expressions. African believers, on the other hand, need no encouragement to use their bodies in worship, and we might admire their lack of inhibitions.

†

We looked earlier at a useful progression – from thanksgiving, to praise, to worship – and music can make sensitive contributions to this journey.

Musicians will understand that such things as speed, timing, rhythm, melody, harmony, volume and silence can all inhibit or enhance our worship.

This need not be complicated. How many times have songs/hymns been driven along so quickly that it has been impossible to draw breath, let alone contemplate the words! And songs sung in the wrong key are also usually unhelpful – requiring the human voice to descend or ascend beyond its normal range.

As Solomon said, "To everything there is a season, and a time for every matter" [Eccl.3:1]:

- a time for the pipe organ or drums to 'let rip';
- a time for the violin to speak into worshipful silence;
- a time for human voices to be unaccompanied;
- a time for rich harmonies to enhance our songs;
- a time for rhythm to get us dancing;
- a time for kneeling in silence;
- a time for solo voices;
- a time for choirs;
- a time for musical simplicity;
- a time for orchestral extravagance.

Worship can be instrumental as well as vocal – instruments playing to the Lord for His praise and glory. Individuals or small groups of musicians can experience the joy of playing directly to the Lord, led by the Spirit and without musical notation or planning.

On several occasions those involved have said things like, "Where did that come from?" when the inspiration has finally died down. On just one occasion the author has been privileged to hear and watch a whole orchestra playing in the Spirit and without human direction. Truly amazing!

There is also the gift of singing to the Lord, sometimes in tongues and sometimes not, when voices rise to create music which is inspired from heaven.

In Search of Worship

Music can express every emotion and enrich our worship in so many ways.

†

Can there be any higher use for music than to be the vehicle which lifts our worship into the heavenly realm? Surely not!

In summary, we can say that whilst so much of present-day music serves commerce and provides us with entertainment, music will always have an eternal role in expressing our thanksgiving and worship, and that its highest purpose will always be God-focussed – in both time and eternity.

24

Cultural Contexts

We began this book with some questions, one of which asked if worship would be expressed differently in different cultures.

The answer is for the most part yes, but not entirely.

We have established that worship is an expression of love and is not an entity in itself.

We can therefore ask how love expresses itself in differing cultures. Despite some minor variations, it is probably true to say that there are common factors in the ways people show their love for each other. Hugging, kissing, touching, smiling and, of course, sexual acts surpass all cultural traditions and are understood by most people groups.

To my knowledge there are no cultures in which love is expressed by pinching noses, kissing kneecaps, head-scratching or turning round three times!

So, expressions of love seem fairly universal and are widely understood.

When it comes to expressing love to the Lord (Whom of course we do not physically see), maybe there are equally common responses which transcend cultures – things like kneeling, lying prostrate, dancing, raising hands, singing, shouting, bowing down, standing silently in awe, or just speaking out our love and appreciation.

Some of those responses will be more common in some cultures than in others, but broadly speaking they will be widely understood.

†

Nonetheless, there are and have been different expressions of worship, both in different parts of the world and in different periods of time.

In Search of Worship

For example, monks in the Middle Ages expressed their worship differently from, say, the Jesus People of the 1960s in America.

Stories have been passed down in the author's family about The Peculiar People (a small denomination which existed in the early 1900s) who were occasionally so excited in their worship that they would leap over the church pews. Whether this was accompanied by singing is not known, and the practice would certainly raise some eyebrows today!

Any Christian converts from the Whirling Dervishes (a Muslim group known for their wild dancing) would express their praise differently from, say, Martin Luther!

King David's tabernacle worship style would probably not naturally express the worship of modern believers, but I often wish we had some CDs of his music, just to be sure!

Speaking of David's worship, dancing in his underwear may not have been his regular worship custom, but it expressed what was in his heart at that time. There is no record of it being repeated by David or anyone else, although zealous courtiers may have considered starting a new denomination where underwear-dancing was obligatory! Certainly, not many church leaders would countenance such behaviour in their 11am services.

David's exuberance pleased the Lord because it was wholeheartedly to Him and not to entertain his subjects or show off his physique. Conversely, his wife's displeasure (however understandable it may have been at the time) was rewarded by barrenness for the rest of her life. There is surely a warning here, that we should not be too quick to judge unusual expressions of worship when they may seem to us to be excessive or unnecessary.

In our day, the cultural differences between various age groups are probably more pronounced than in any previous generation, and this will naturally be reflected in the worship style of differing age groups (although not exclusively so). Different church streams and denominations also tend to produce their own worship styles, although the internet has meant that worship material is widely shared across the world.

†

The key here is not the mode of worship but the heart of love from which it overflows.

If David is an example, almost anything goes, and will be acceptable to God if it expresses genuine love and thanksgiving for all He is and all He does.

So while there will always be culturally-related demonstrations of worship for different people groups, there is also common ground beneath those differences, and we can only imagine what a wealth of diversity will be evident when all earth's people groups gather around the throne and offer their praise and worship.

The synthesis of the worldwide church's expressions of worship will be awesome – all languages, all music genres, music from every century and every age group, all possibly combined with the worship of the stars and all nature!

When that happens, I think our Lord Jesus will (to quote the prophet Isaiah) *"see [the fruit] of the travail of His soul and be satisfied"* [Is.53:11].

25

Evangelism or Worship?

This book may have led some to wonder if a choice has to be made – between spreading the gospel and concentrating on worship. Some may have seen worship as a diversion away from the church's primary task of evangelism. Others, probably fewer in number, may have neglected the 'great commission' and concentrated their focus on worship.

Is there, or should there be, any conflict here? Absolutely not. But an understanding of the relationship between the two seems to be unclear in many places.

We know that many churches focus on evangelism and reaching out to their local communities, and that this absorbs most of their time, their people and their finances. Responding to Jesus' final command – *"Go into all the world and preach ... (the Gospel)"* [Mk.16:15] – is seen as the church's main priority, and worshipping God is, perhaps unconsciously, sidelined.

We should certainly not underestimate the importance of responding to Christ's command, and there is no conflict between evangelism and worship. We should, however, see the goal of evangelism as releasing more worshippers for the glory of God. If we stop short of this goal and see only the 'hell-avoiding' benefits of our salvation, we have missed the point, and will continue to focus on man's needs and not God's glory. Our salvation is much broader than *saved from* – it is, far more gloriously, *saved to*. We need to head new believers toward a life of worship – which should be the goal of maturity and holiness.

This is a long way from the mission statements of some churches, which clearly state that they exist to 'train leaders', and which, by implication, means that they focus on equipping their members to be leaders of other congregations which will then form other congregations who will then... in order to serve people. Whilst the training of leaders is laudable, the goal must surely be to ensure that believers mature into worshipping members of God's family – whilst also affecting their communities with demonstrations of God's love.

If the purpose of evangelism is man-centred, it will not extend to its ultimate purpose of glorifying God and will produce believers who see salvation as a 'rescue from' opportunity and not a 'release into' the eternal purposes of God.

Clear teaching about, and the opportunity for, worship will ensure that churches do not settle for less than their high calling and minister only to the needs of men. The author is aware of churches which have sidelined worship and gradually dwindled away.

God's purpose in forming the church (*ecclesia* = 'the called out ones') is not primarily for the purpose of evangelistic activity. We are *called to demonstrate* as well as *commissioned to declare*.

The life-changing truth of the Gospel needs to be broadcast to the ends of the earth, and God, in His wisdom, has ordained that this involves preaching [1Cor.1:21]. But is it easy to overlook the end product and see only the process by which this is achieved.

Even if the Gospel resulted in the salvation of every living person, this in itself would not represent the completion of God's purposes. God's goal is greater than rescuing all men from an eternity in hell.

"...He raised us up ... with Christ ... [giving us joint seating with Him] in the heavenly sphere ... so that He might clearly demonstrate through the ages to come the immeasurable ... riches of His ... grace" [Eph.2:6-7].

The church "continues to rise ... into a holy temple in the Lord [a sanctuary dedicated ... to the presence of the Lord]" [Eph.2.21].

God's "[purpose is] that through the church the many-sided wisdom of God ... might now be made known to the angelic rulers and ... (principalities ...) in the heavenly sphere" [Eph.3.10].

Our salvation is a means to an end – and the end is God's glory, not our safety! So if we only see our task as working toward the salvation of men, we will have fallen short of seeing God's eternal plan.

In Search of Worship

One consequence of this limited perspective is that we can assume that God's glory depends on our diligence and efforts. We must therefore work hard to publicise God's cause and ensure that the Gospel is understood by as many as possible! This is of course partially true, but… The 'but' refers to the fact that God's power is not limited to the success or otherwise of our evangelistic output, and His goal is greater than anything we can achieve.

If we focussed more often on offering up our worship to Him, would His coming down to inhabit our praises achieve far more than much of the horizontal activity we carry out on His behalf? As suggested earlier, the presence of light is the most effective way of dispelling darkness!

†

It is also interesting to note that God's chosen people, Israel, were never commissioned as a missionary nation. They were not tasked with converting the surrounding nations.

"Now therefore, if you will obey My voice … and keep My covenant, then you shall be My own peculiar possession and treasure … above all peoples. …you shall be to Me a kingdom of priests, a holy nation [… set apart to the worship of God]" [Ex.19:5-6].

Had they remained faithful to their God, His provision for them would have been a powerful demonstration to surrounding nations that Israel's God was superior to all others – and worth worshipping.

To the extent that they worshipped God, He blessed them, and His blessings were evidence of His identity and power. Their faithful worship was the key to their effectiveness as 'witnesses' to God's existence. Can we learn from this?

†

The apostle Peter, writing to believers (including Gentiles) scattered around Asia, echoes the same though when speaking about the church: *"But you are a chosen race, a royal priesthood, a dedicated nation, [God's] … special people, that you may … display the virtues and perfections of Him Who called you out of darkness into His marvelous light"* [1Pet.2:9].

Evangelism or Worship?

We are indeed commissioned to declare the gospel – but, more than that, we are to be evidence of God's glory by being a royal priesthood, demonstrating His faithfulness and offering acceptable worship to Him. We are called to be more than servants promoting the gospel. We are to function as a royal priesthood in a loving relationship with the God Who called us out of darkness.

As mentioned previously, when Jesus was about to commission Peter to evangelise, He first ensured that Peter had a love relationship with Him. He also honoured His disciples by calling them friends and not just servants.

†

In responding to Jesus' command to *"Go..."* the disciples did not cease to be worshipping believers.

Locked in a prison several years later, Paul and Silas spent their time worshipping their Lord – with incredible side effects! Presumably this was a normal part of their lives and not just a panic response to a difficult situation!

†

Although this chapter looks primarily at what some people may perceive as a conflict between worship and evangelism, the issue is actually broader than this.

The story of Mary and Martha illustrates a wider point [Lk.10:38]. You probably know the story: Martha was busy preparing a meal while Mary sat at Jesus' feet – enjoying His presence and listening to His teaching. Martha was serving. Mary was apparently lazy!

Who got it right? Neither or both? Martha understood that there is a time to be serving the Lord. Mary understood that there is a time to lay down the oven cloth and be in His presence.

Spending time 'serving' the Lord is both necessary and commended (*"Well done, good and faithful servant,"* [Matt.25:21] according to Jesus' story), but there is also a time to cease 'serving', and to prioritise His presence. Similarly, we need to understand that 'serving the Lord' should not eclipse our high calling to be worshippers.

In Search of Worship

We have already looked at the incredible revelation which Jesus shared with the woman at the well – that His Father is seeking worshippers. He is looking for those who will worship Him in spirit and truth. We might imagine that if God needed to seek anything, it might be for qualified workers to bring in His kingdom, but Jesus draws the woman's attention to the fact that His Father is actively seeking those who will worship Him in spirit and truth. This alone should alert us to the importance of worshipping Him.

When Jesus was about to commission Peter to *"Feed My sheep"*, He first ensured that Peter had a love relationship with Him [Jn.21:17].

So, worship, practical service and evangelism need not be seen as conflicting entities, even though in practice it may not be easy for us to divide our time and resources between them.

Individually we are all called to be worshippers, as well as being involved in spreading the good news of the Gospel.

Corporately, as Christ's church, we are called to be a worshipping community as well as a working community.

26

Summary and Conclusion

We have looked at various aspects of worship – some in more detail than others – and have asked some challenging questions on the way.

The aim of this book has been to inspire and not just to inform. Hopefully, it will release you as a worshipper (and perhaps those you lead) into new dimensions of worship which will exalt our wonderful Lord even more highly – because He is worth it!

Our search for biblical worship has taken us on a journey, during which we have paused to consider the following:

- We looked at the words we use, and asked what defines true worship.
- We saw that worship continues beyond time and space, and that worship of anything apart from God is idolatry.
- We reviewed early examples of worship in Scripture, and saw that worship versus idolatry was God's primary concern when giving His people the Law.
- We asked what it meant to *"serve"* God after leaving Egypt, and saw that throughout Scripture the word used means 'to minister to', not 'to work for'.
- We understood that the purpose of releasing the people from Egypt was not primarily for their comfort but in order that they could worship Him, and that God's purpose in setting us free from the bondage of sin is that we might focus on Him and be worshippers.
- We looked briefly at tabernacle worship and the symbolic ark of the covenant.
- The Psalms helped us to understand that there can be a progression in our worship – of approaching with thanksgiving, offering our

praise and entering into the intimacy of His presence with our worship.

- We looked at David, the shepherd turned king, who probably understood worship more than any other biblical character and who left us a legacy of worship material.
- We asked the question, "Why should we worship God?"
- There are many hindrances to worship and we looked briefly at a few.
- We emphasised that true worship must be *to* Him and not just *about* Him, and saw that, sadly, much Christian music falls into the latter category.
- We marvelled at the scope and detail of David's preparations for worship in the temple which his son Solomon would build – including the appointment of four thousand singers and musicians.
- We summarised instances of worship in the New Testament and noted the glimpses of heavenly worship which the apostle John saw on Patmos.
- We examined the Christian songs we sing and asked how many of them constitute worship.
- We explored some of the things that happen when we worship God.
- We warned of the dangers of having ulterior motives for worshipping.
- We briefly looked at some of the enemy's strategies for preventing our worship.
- We saw that music has been used in many contexts and how it has now been devalued by popular use and in commercial enterprise.
- We noted that there is a connection between worship and tithing and saw that the priests needed to be adequately supported from the sacrificial gifts of the people, enabling them to carry out their duties. We asked how many churches value worship enough to set aside resources for those involved.
- We saw the significance of 'journey' in worship, in our spiritual 'journey' into the presence of God.

†

Many of the issues raised in this book will impact on the church formats that presently exist and within which many of us function.

Services which are strictly liturgical and repeatedly follow the same format can be restrictive in facilitating corporate worship, although some may find this helpful. However there are examples of liturgical structure which successfully incorporate times of free worship, and this is encouraging.

In recent years there have been parachurch gatherings where times of worship have been given a higher priority, with less time constraints than is normal in a regular service. In such a context, it is easier to employ some of the guidelines set out in this book.

Since the Reformation in England, considerable priority has been given to the preaching and teaching of Scripture – both in the design and layout of our church buildings and in the format of our services. Everything leads up to the main event, which is a presentation from the pulpit, expounding Scripture or giving moral guidance. In this format, worship is usually minimal and often little understood. Embracing some of the principles set out in this book will require the allocation of more time to worship, and we understand that this will not be possible in the context of many meetings. Some groups provide opportunities for more sustained times of worship outside the regular service events, and it is easier to explore new depths of worship in this format.

The availability of skilled and sensitive musicians to lead and accompany worship is another factor – not essential, of course, but usually helpful. We may dream of king David's four thousand dedicated singers and musicians, but in reality we may be alone or with just a few others. Of course, the Lord appreciates true worship whether it comes from the many or the few, and whether it has musical accompaniment or not. Undoubtedly, He enjoyed David's solo worship alone with his sheep just as much as the perfected offerings of the huge temple choir. But the availability of skilled musicians whose hearts are set on glorifying God and not their own talents will always be helpful and inspiring.

†

We face many challenges if we are to ensure that worshipping our Lord remains a priority. Worship will always be highly contested. The enemy hates the presence of Almighty God, and the fact that God promises to inhabit our praises is bound to stir up the enemy's anger. Whilst we may 'move mountains' and achieve much by our prayers and devoted service, His powerful presence in times of worship can also have miraculous consequences.

†

It is worth repeating that true worship springs out of love not duty.

Moses' tabernacle was constructed only from the people's offerings which were given willingly and ungrudgingly [Ex.25]. God wanted His worship centre to be built from freely-given materials and not reluctant offerings! All the subsequent regulations and instructions sprung from this foundation – that His people had freely and willingly contributed to the place of worship.

Likewise, worship is our privilege and not a legal requirement!

Solomon's temple was constructed from massive blocks of stone, hewn from quarries and individually sculpted to fit together before they were transported to the temple site. Archaeologists have been amazed at the accuracy of the work and the precise jointing of the stones. As believers we too are being fashioned right now as *"living stones"* to form part of a spiritual temple [1Pet.2:5].

In God's master plan, each of us has an individual identity and function which will contribute to a vast worship cathedral for all eternity, once we are brought together around His throne! What a calling!

May God inspire and richly bless you as you explore new heights and depths in worship.

"Blessed ... are those who dwell in Your house and Your presence; they will be singing Your praises all day long. ... They go from strength to strength..."

Psalm 84:4,7

"...sing to the Lord; ... make a joyful noise to the Rock of our salvation! ...come before His presence with thanksgiving; ... make a joyful noise to Him with songs of praise!"

Psalm 95:1-2

About the Author

John Clements grew up in a Christian home and his relationship with the Lord began at an early age. He has been involved in churches and in church music since childhood, as were both his parents, to whom he owes a great deal.

He has been privileged to serve the Lord in various capacities over several decades, in the UK and beyond, including oversight of worship, eldership, responsibility for oversees mission, and as co-leader of a community church. More recently he and his wife helped to set up a facility which was dedicated solely to worship – a place where anyone could come and spend time worshipping the Lord. It was in this context that much of the inspiration for the material in this book began to unfold, as the Lord 'inhabited' the praises of His people.

The author's passion for worship and love of quality music combine in this book as he encourages us to ensure that our offerings of worship are worthy of the One Who paid such a high price for our salvation.

The author may be contacted by email:

john423clements@gmail.com

More information about the author can be found on the book's web page:

www.onwardsandupwards.org/**in-search-of-worship**